IN PRAISE OF

CHICKENS

A Compendium of Wisdom
Fair and Fowl

JANE S. SMITH

Lyons Press
Guilford, Connecticut
An imprint of Globe Pequot Press

Copyright © 2012 by Jane S. Smith

Lyons Press is an imprint of Globe Pequot Press.

Text design: Georgiana Goodwin

Library of Congress Cataloging-in-Publication Data is available on file.

ISBN 978-0-7627-7350-3

Printed in China

10 9 8 7 6 5 4 3 2 1

*To all the chicken fanciers, egg finders, feather collectors,
barnyard experts, backyard observers, armchair poultry
enthusiasts, and passionate amateurs who are changing
the world, one henhouse at a time.*

Fowls are a Stock the poorest may keep, and such as the richest need not to neglect; they are universal, and they very well deserve to be so.

—Thomas Hale, *A Compleat Body of Husbandry*, 1758

CONTENTS

Introduction: The Cluck Heard Round the World   vi

On Names: Who's Who in the Henhouse   I

A Brief History of Chickens: Domesticating Tyrannosaurus Rex   3

On Hens: Don't Mess with Mama   13

On Roosters: Cock of the Walk   21

On Capons: Plump Pacifists of the Poultry Yard   31

On Breeds: My Favorite Chicken   35

Secret Arts: Laying, Hatching, and Preserving Eggs   49

Cooped Up: Building a Palace for Your Poultry   71

In Sickness and in Health: Protecting Chickens Through the Ages   79

Count Your Chickens: The Numerology of Flock and Nest   91

Dumb Clucks and Birdbrains: Can a Chicken Beat You at Checkers?   97

When in Doubt, Ask a Chicken: Poultry for Seekers and Believers   III

The Chicken as Muse: Poultry for Poets and Philosophers   119

Fine-Feathered Friends: Chickens as Pets   125

Rules of the Roost: Chickens and the Law   133

Fun with Eggs: How to Play with Your Food   137

Parting Advice: Instructions for Beginning Chicken Keepers   140

Bonus Readings: Harriet Beecher Stowe and Mark Twain Visit the Henhouse   141

Acknowledgments and Note on Sources   160

Illustration Credits   164

INTRODUCTION:

The Cluck Heard Round the World

Why chickens?

A better question is, why not chickens? What animal is more worthy of our attention, our affection, and our curiosity?

Useful and portable, chickens have traveled from their origins in the jungles of Southeast Asia to every place of human settlement on earth. There were chickens in China before the arrival of Buddha, chickens in Palestine before Jesus, roosters carved in Egyptian cameos when Cleopatra sailed the Nile, and hens that laid blue eggs in southern Chile long before Spaniards brought European poultry to what they called the New World. In 1774, when Captain Cook arrived on Easter Island, the most remote habitable place on the planet, he marveled at the gigantic stone heads—and the domesticated chickens.

For most of human history, chickens have been a familiar part of every household, humble and grand. In the twentieth century, the family flock became a thing of the past, but that seems to be changing. Everywhere we look, a growing number of people seems to be obsessed with chickens. Many are raising chickens, or hoping to raise chickens, or thinking about moving to larger quarters so they could begin to hope to raise chickens. Others are spending enormous sums on poultry that, prior to becoming dinner, lead lives most of us can only wish for: fed organically, ranging freely, and even, according to a sign I saw in a small grocery store, "hand-petted every day in Bodega Bay."

That was in California, as it happened, but it could have been anywhere. After decades of neglect, chickens are once again taking their proper place at the center of popular attention. The desire for fresh-laid eggs, preferably from a hen you know by name, has moved from eccentricity to eco-sophistication. From the new restaurant that prides itself on serving only locally sourced food to the urban homesteader crafting a henhouse next to the back stairs, the cluck of the chicken has become the anthem for a return to a more intimate, less industrialized relationship with nature, with other creatures, and (at least for carnivores) with food.

Observing this resurgent interest in poultry, I began to wonder how earlier generations had thought about the chickens in their midst. So I did what history-minded people do: I went to the library. Specifically, the rare book library. I buttonholed curators, pestered experts for translations from the Latin, pored over scientific treatises and agricultural how-to books of prior centuries, and dug through collections of rare and often beautiful advertising ephemera. The result? Treasures too wonderful not to share.

As far as I can tell, people have been studying chickens, revering chickens, consulting chickens, offering advice on caring for chickens, and compiling lavishly illustrated treatises disputing other people's advice about chickens, since shortly after the discovery of the first egg. Every age has produced its experts and enthusiasts, from Aristotle investigating chicken embryos in ancient Greece and Pliny the Elder reporting on roosters from first-century Rome to Athanasius Kircher's 1546 demonstration of how to hypnotize a chicken and the 1912 compilers of a twenty-three word dictionary of chicken language. What they all share is the conviction that there is nothing so consistently engrossing as watching chickens being themselves—unless, perhaps, it is listening to other people talk about chickens.

What follows is a small sampling of this rich history of poultry lore, a compact collection of art, literature, natural history, religion, and (let's be honest) general silliness gathered from the works of poets, philosophers, scientists, and dreamers as well as "practical" experts. Early authors and their translators have been quoted with their antique spelling intact. Entries are organized by topic, not period, so readers can compare authorities from different epochs as they air their opinions on all things chicken.

Well, not quite all things. There is nothing here about cockfighting or the modern poultry industry. There are no recipes, either, or at least none that seem safe to eat. Not every note that follows is entirely reliable—readers who try to ward off an attacking lion by brandishing a cockscomb do so at their own risk. But much of the wisdom of the past is still applicable, and all of it is fun.

Full disclosure: I don't have any chickens at the moment, but I have kept chickens in my day. I have fed them, watered them, gathered their eggs, interceded in their quarrels, worried about their health, and even, one dismal day, accidentally run over a bantam rooster who wanted to pick a fight with my car. All of which is to say, I understand the passion, the joy, and the madness of those in the grip of hen fever.

THE POULTRY OF THE WORLD

Portraits of all known valuable breeds of fowls

ON NAMES

Who's Who in the Henhouse

Before the nineteenth century, the name *chicken* was reserved for very young birds, and any general reference to what we now call chickens was *fowl*. Here are some other names that are useful to know:

Chick: a newly hatched chicken.

Pullet: a young female.

Hen: a mature female, ready to lay eggs.

Biddy: an older hen, no longer good for laying but sometimes excellent for hatching and watching over young chicks.

Cockerel: a young male.

Cock: a mature male.

Rooster: a genteel name for a cock, introduced in the nineteenth century and most popular in the United States.

Capon: a cockerel that has been castrated so he will grow into a very large bird (not done very often these days).

Chook: Australian name for chickens.

Utility chicken: any breed raised for meat or eggs, not for show. Also called *plain*.

Fancy: attractive breeds, often with exotic feathers, prized for display and competition in poultry shows. Many chicken lovers raise both plain and fancy.

Gallus gallus domesticus: under Linnaean classification, the scientific name for the common domestic chicken.

Silver Spangled Polands

A BRIEF HISTORY OF CHICKENS

Domesticating Tyrannosaurus Rex

Did chickens evolve from dinosaurs? It's an attractive theory, which is what we call something that is not quite proved but fun to imagine. The word "evolve" derives from the Latin for "out of the egg," after all, and at least some dinosaurs had feathers, wings, and probably beaks. Recent molecular studies of dinosaur protein suggest that chickens may be the closest genetic descendent of the fierce *Tyrannosaurus rex*, a fact that won't surprise anyone who has watched a hen attack a hapless worm.

The more immediate ancestor of the modern chicken was the wild red junglefowl, probably interbred with the grey junglefowl—species that survive today and bear a striking resemblance to the colorful creatures known as the *common*, *barnyard*, or *dunghill* fowl. From Thailand, Vietnam, and Southeast Asia, the birds migrated to China and Egypt and then to India, Persia, and Greece. Somewhere along the way, they were domesticated. Howard Carter, the archeologist famous for his 1923 discovery of the tomb of Tutankhamun, also uncovered what he considered "the earliest known drawing of the domestic cock," made during the reign of Tutmose III some time between 1479 and 1425 BCE. Archeological remains of domesticated chickens date back much longer, perhaps as long as ten thousand years, making them among the first animal species willing and able to live among humans.

As for the question of which came first, the chicken or the egg, the debate continues. Strict readers of Genesis favor the chicken, since God created "every winged fowl" on the fifth day. Greek philosopher Aristotle also said the chicken came first, though Plato disagreed. In Hindu theology, all creation—chickens, humans, trees, grass, the entire universe—emerged from the cosmic egg. Charles Darwin defended the precedence of the egg, arguing that the modern chicken first appeared from an embryonic mutation,

before hatching. In 2010, however, researchers at Sheffield and Warwick universities in England argued that the chicken must take precedence, since eggs do not form shells in the absence of specific proteins that only a hen can provide. A conclusive answer is nowhere in sight.

Whatever their origins, chickens have traveled the world by hitching rides on the roads of conquest. The Dorking, for example, is honored as the definitive heirloom breed of England, but this distinctive, five-toed bird almost certainly arrived in Britain with Julius Caesar's Roman army, which in turn had brought it north from Egypt. Spanish sailors kept chickens in coops on deck when they sailed to the western hemisphere; before they arrived in Mexico, chickens were unknown in North America, as were horses. The horse opened up much wider hunting grounds, but proved to be an expensive addition to any domestic budget. Chickens, able to scratch about for much of their food, became a welcome part of humbler, more stationary households.

By the middle of the nineteenth century, the ordinary barnyard chicken became part of the transcontinental migration in which so much of the North American population moved west. During the California Gold

Rush, when the surest way of finding a fortune was to sell supplies to the hordes of gold seekers, a single egg might command three dollars (half a week's pay for many workers) in a mining camp. The leader of a group of would-be prospectors reported the following in his diary when crossing the foothills of the Sierra Nevada Mountains:

October 13, 1849
We now make a short and stony ascent, and turned left, (Easterly) crossed a hollow—where was an Irishman & his wife, with an ox-wagon, to the rear of which was attached a large hen-coop, full of *chickens* and *roosters*. And Pat swore by the *"howly mother of Moses,"* that he'd starve before he'd kill one of 'em: intending to make a grand speculation in California on them.

—J. Goldsborough Bruff, *Gold Rush*, 1849

Another group of Gold Rush adventurers found the people of Sante Fe, New Mexico, using a chicken to adapt old-world amusements to their new environment. Here we see an event that is a cross between a rodeo and a game of tag.

The 24th of June (Sunday) was a great day at Santa Fe. All of the people assembled in the grand plaza, and turned a chicken loose. Some 500 men mounted on horses, mules, and jackasses, took after the chicken, and then gave chase through the streets after the man who had the chicken. They kept this up till night, the Priest being amongst the crowd and enjoying the sport as much as any of them.

—Letter from California Emigrants,
Arkansas State Democrat, 1849

Partridge Cochin

Meanwhile, in Europe and the more settled parts of the United States, cultivating ornamental chickens was becoming a fashionable hobby. New breeds from China and Japan began to arrive in England in the 1840s, and poultry keepers with disposable income were gripped by a passionate desire to collect and exhibit them, particularly the large Shanghai or Cochin-China birds with heavily feathered legs. The first poultry show in North America, held on Boston Common in 1849, excited a frenzy of competitive breeding and spiraling poultry prices that many likened to the tulip mania of seventeenth-century Holland. One of the first to profit, first by selling rare specimens and then by publishing a very popular book satirizing the craze, was George Burnham:

> Never in the history of modern "bubbles," probably, did any mania exceed in ridiculousness or ludicrousness, or in the number of its victims surpass this inexplicable humbug, the "hen fever."
> . . . The press of the country, far and near, was alive with accounts of "extraordinary pullets," "enormous eggs" (laid on the tables of the editors), "astounding prices" obtained for individual

specimens of rare poultry; and all sorts of people, of every trade and profession and calling in life, were on the *qui vive*, and joined in the hue-and-cry, regarding the suddenly and newly ascertained fact that hens laid eggs.

—George P. Burnham,
The History of the Hen Fever, 1855

Even when prices declined, the passion for poultry shows continued, and prize specimens of cocks and hens became a coveted status symbol for the new breed of chicken fanciers. In England, where the zeal for all manner of collections was already well developed, Queen Victoria cherished her poultry. In 1860, when the British army invaded Peking and sacked the emperor's Summer Palace, several very pretty bantam chickens were part of the spoils presented to Her Royal Highness.

By the start of the twentieth century, as more people lived in urban centers, keeping chickens and other livestock was often restricted by local statute. It was only after the Second World War, though, that the small family chicken farm gave way to much larger operations and the chicken coop for home use vanished from the yard.

Today, there are more chickens on earth than any other species of bird, and at least three times as many chickens as humans, but much of this population lives in crowded cages on giant factory farms. Too often, the only chicken that modern consumers encounter is thoroughly denatured—skinned, boned, shredded, breaded, and even processed into nuggets shaped like the dinosaurs from which it may have evolved.

We've never quite lost our old familiarity, though, with this most common of birds. References to household chickens continue to roost in our language and perch in our decorative landscape. We still speak of an escapee as someone who *flew the coop*, reject a paltry sum as *chicken feed* and bad handwriting as *chicken scratchings* (or, in Dutch, *hennescraps*), and describe a social hierarchy as *the pecking order*. When we put aside money we hope will fund the start of some grand enterprise, we call it a *nest egg*, after the glass or china decoys used to persuade a hen to start laying. A man whose pride exceeds his size or his abilities is *cocky*, men bossed around or belittled by their wives are *hen-pecked*, and attractive young women are *chicks* while older ones are sometimes dismissed as *biddies* or *no spring chickens*. Kitchens continue to be full of objects decorated with images of roosters and hens that few of us, until recently, have had a chance to see alive.

Take heart. The authentic chicken, that clucking egg producer and gorgeous, crowing herald of the sun, is making a comeback. People everywhere are rediscovering the complex pleasures of keeping chickens. In 1928, Herbert Hoover's presidential campaign boasted of "Republican prosperity" that promised a chicken in every pot and also a car in every garage. What followed was not prosperity, but the financial crash of 1929 and a decade of global hardship known as the Great Depression.

How much better it would have been if they had promised a chicken in every garage. It might still happen. And that would be something to crow about.

Partridge Cochin Hen

ON HENS

Don't Mess with Mama

Before poultry became a year-round industry, hens rarely laid or hatched eggs in the winter, and a spring chicken remains synonymous with everything tender and young. Hens over three or four years old, kept alive out of affection or to serve as substitute nurses for the chicks of younger hens, often ruled the henhouse, and the old biddy is still considered an emblem of bossy interference. But it is the middle stage of a hen's life that has inspired the most tributes.

The mother hen is a paragon of domesticity. In the popular children's story of *The Little Red Hen*, the heroine takes on all the duties of a good farmer when her lazy barnyard comrades will not help her cultivate the grain of wheat she finds; she plants, harvests, threshes, grinds, and bakes the grain to make bread to feed her chicks, and makes sure they get to eat it undisturbed. But there's no need to put a hen in an apron to show her devotion to home and brood, as the following writers knew.

We daily behold hens, how they cherish their chickens, taking some of them under their spread wings, suffering others of them to run upon their backs, and taking them in again, with a voice expressing kindness and joy. When themselves are concerned, they fly from dogs and serpents; but to defend their chickens, they will venture beyond their strength and fight.

—Plutarch, *On Affection for Offspring*, c. 70 AD

Sultans

How with greate love the wanton hen doth keepe
A houshold bird, and warde her tender broode.
If from house top the swift hawk toe peep
Shee stands upright and voice doth cackle loude,
And calling she doth bring
Her chirping babes under her swelling wynge
—Edward Topsell, *The Fowles of Heaven*, 1614

She leads them forward where they are likely to have the greatest quantity of grain, and takes care to show, by pecking, the sort proper for them to seek for. Though at other times voracious, she is then abstemious to an extreme degree, and intent only on providing for, and showing her young clutch their food, she scarce takes any nourishment herself. Her parental pride seems to overpower every other appetite.

—Oliver Goldsmith, *A History of the Earth and Animated Nature*, 1774

Dark Brahma Pullet

The Hen is deservedly the acknowledged pattern of maternal love. When her passion of philoprogenitiveness is disappointed by the failure or subtraction of her own brood, she will either go on sitting till her natural powers fail, or will violently kidnap the young of other Fowls, and insist upon adopting them.

—Edmund Saul Dixon,
Ornamental and Domestic Poultry, 1848

Like all good mothers, hens tend to the spiritual as well as the physical needs of their children, at least according to Roman authorities.

The Hens of Country-houses possess some Religion. When they have laid an Egg they fall a trembling, and shake themselves. They turn about, also, to be purified, and with some Sprigs of a Bush they purify by Lustration [sprinkling with water] themselves and their Eggs.

—Pliny the Elder, *Natural History*, 79 AD

Hens may be wonderful mothers, but they are not dainty creatures. Gilbert White, an English country parson who was also one of the great naturalists of the eighteenth century, understood the fierceness of a hen's emotions.

> March 16, 1776: [Maternal love] sublimes the passions, quickens the invention, and sharpens the sagacity of the brute creation. Thus a hen, just become a mother, is no longer that placid bird she used to be, but with feathers standing on end, wings hovering, and clocking note, she runs about like one possessed.
> —Gilbert White, *Natural History of Selborne*, 1789

In the early twentieth century, the editors of the *Larousse Encyclopedia of Domestic Life (Larousse Ménager)*

explored the psychology of the female chicken with the same acute attention to hidden passions that novelist Marcel Proust applied to the secrets of the human heart:

> Beneath their modest and peaceful exteriors, hens hide a somewhat turbulent character. They can be heard constantly chattering and quarreling among themselves. One can also blame them for a certain amount of cruelty. If one of their flock is sick, or wounded, they unite to finish it off. When a newcomer enters the barnyard, they give her a poor welcome, overwhelm her with blows, and keep up their hostilities for several days unless she is given special protection from the cock, the lord and master of the place.
>
> —*Larousse Encyclopedia of Domestic Life*, 1926

When farmers become soldiers, food quickly becomes a strategic commodity. Napoleon famously observed that an army travels on its stomach, and eggs are often rationed when a country goes to war. During the First World War, hens were enlisted to serve on the home front and were even shown in uniform in the posters that were such a large part of national food production campaigns on both sides of the Atlantic.

Poultry wasn't rationed during World War II, but at the height of the Victory Garden movement, in 1943, the world's largest department store opened what they called the Macy's Victory Barnyard, selling live chickens and all their accessories in the heart of New York City.

Combed Dorking

ON ROOSTERS
Cock of the Walk

The cock is a fighter, a lover, and a doting husband and father. He is a model for the industrious early riser but also seen by some as the incarnation of vanity, pride, and recklessness. European churches often have roosters on their weathervanes as guardians of the spiritual flock. And yet, like many other boys, the rooster is often criticized simply for being himself: noisy, brash, and prone to breaking things. Today the cock is often banished from the backyard coop, but the future of poultry depends on his presence.

Early observers credited the rooster with the ability to terrorize much larger animals, as shown in the following passage from Lucretius, written a half-century before the birth of Christ.

> *Lo, the raving lions,*
> *They dare not face and gaze upon the cock*
> *Who's wont with wings to flap away the night*
> *From off the stage, and call the beaming morn*
> *With clarion voice—and lions straightway thus*
> *Bethink themselves of flight, because, ye see,*

Within the body of the cocks there be
Some certain seeds, which, into lions' eyes
Injected, bore into the pupils deep
And yield such piercing pain they can't hold out
Against the cocks, however fierce they be.
—Lucretius, *On the Nature of Things*, 50 BCE

Pliny the Elder, the Roman historian and naturalist who died trying to observe the volcanic destruction of Pompeii, also admired the rooster as a warrior in feathers:

The lion, so fierce as he is, is . . . terrified of the Cock's Comb, and much more with his Crowing.

At Pergamus every Year there is an Exhibition publicly afforded to the People, of Cocks, as of Gladiators.

—Pliny, *Natural History*, 79 AD

Fifteen hundred years later, the rooster was still famed and feared for his power over dark and ominous forces. In *Hamlet*, Shakespeare cites the rooster's ability to vanquish ghosts and other spirits, and repeats the legend that the cock, "the bird of dawning," crows throughout the night before Christmas.

Some say that ever, 'gainst that season comes
Wherein our Saviour's birth is celebrated,
The bird of dawning singeth all night long;
And then, they say, no spirit dare stir abroad,
The nights are wholesome, then no planets strike,
No fairy takes, nor witch hath power to charm,
So hallow'd and so gracious is the time.
—William Shakespeare, *Hamlet*, 1601

Fearsome as he can be, the rooster is also admired as a model for the family man.

WEDDED MAN'S JUDGMENT
As cock that wants his mate, goes roving all about,
With crowing early and late, to find his lover out;
And as poore sillie hen, long wanting cock to guide,
Soone droopes, and shortly then beginnes to peake aside;

Even so it is with man and wife, where government is found.
The want of t'one, the other's (a) life, doth shortly soone
confound.

—Thomas Tusser, *Five hundred points of good*
husbandry, 1580

The rooster fights because he does not wish any of his hens to be touched by anyone and thus he performs the function of a wise father of a family, appearing to be doing nothing more than to protect his honor. Indeed, he follows his hens with so much love that if they happen to die he pines away from grief.

—Ulisse Aldrovandi, *Ornithology,* 1599

You shall understand that the dunghill-Cocke . . . is a Fowle of all other birds the most manliest, stately, and majesticall, very tame and familiar with the Man. . . . He delighteth in open and liberal plaines, where he may lead forth his Hens into greene pastures, and under hedges, where they may worme and bathe themselves in the sunne.

—Gervaise Markham,
Cheape and Good Husbandry, 1614

The Cock is very attentive to his females, hardly every losing sight of them; he leads, defends, and cherishes them, collects them together when they straggle, and seems to eat unwillingly till he sees them feeding around him.

—Thomas Bewick, *A History of British Birds*, 1805

The busy rooster with his harem of hens has long been an exemplar of sexual prowess.

It is not expedient to keep any cocks for hens, but such as are exceeding salacious.

—Columella, *Of Husbandry*, c. 65 AD

As far as the wantonness of the bird is concerned I should even believe the story about that young rooster which, they say, while she was already carrying Tiberius in her womb, laid an egg in Livia's hand. When she sought to discover whether she would bear a male child or not, she placed the egg under a hen for hatching. Now she, now her servants warmed the egg by hand until a young rooster was hatched out of it. Not only did he portent by his sex the bird of Tiberius, as many insist, but also that salaciousness and impudence which soon made him most notorious. Indeed, whoever has a concave nose, a round forehead, and a round, prominent head like roosters is commonly considered to be fond of sex.

—Ulisse Aldrovandi, *Ornithology*, 1599

He ought, withal, to be brisk, spirited, ardent, and ready in caressing the hens, quick in defending them, attentive in soliciting them to eat, in keeping them together, and in assembling them at night.

—Martin Doyle,
*A Cyclopaedia of Practical Husbandry
and Rural Affairs in General*, 1851

A shy and gentle cock is worthless.

—*Larousse Encyclopedia of Domestic Life*, 1926

Around the world, there is remarkable agreement in different languages on how a rooster crows.

cock-a-doodle-doo (English)
quiquiriqui (Spanish)
cocorico (French)
titilaok (Filipino)
kikeriki (German)
chicchirichi (Italian)
kukarekat (Russian)
kukuriku (Hebrew)
kunguru (Swahili)
kikirikati (Slovenian)
kokekoko (Japanese)
kuukukuuku (Arabic)

But do all roosters crow alike? Charles Darwin didn't think so.

The Malays have a loud, deep, somewhat prolonged crow, but with considerable individual differences. Colonel Sykes remarks that the domestic Kulm cock in India has not the shrill clear pipe of the English bird, and "his scale of notes appears more limited." Dr. Hooker was struck with the "prolonged howling screech" of the cocks in Sikhim. The crow of the Cochin is notoriously and ludicrously different from that of the common cock.

—Charles Darwin, *Variations of Animals and Plants Under Domestication*, 1868

As for the rooster's reputation as a dandy, or cockscomb:

The cock is fond of cleanliness, and very careful of the appearance of his plumes, and hence he may be frequently observed pruning and dressing his feathers with his bill.

—Walter B. Dickson, *Poultry: Their Breeding, Rearing, Diseases, and General Management*, 1838

Many municipalities today allow hens but prohibit roosters, which creates obvious problems for any home fancier who wants fertile eggs for hatching or eating. In truth, the rooster has been threatened for decades. Here is some blunt advice from almost a century ago:

On nearly every farm there are altogether too many cocks kept which are useless except for a brief time during the breeding season, and these help to swell the feed bill, without any return. Fatten the superfluous cockerels and eat them.

—Reese V. Hicks, *New Country Life*, 1918

Minorcas

Dark Brahma

ON CAPONS
Plump Pacifists of the Poultry Yard

Capons are male chickens neutered before they reach maturity, a process that was once very common. In past centuries, the capon was valued as a bird that was easily fattened for the table and also as a substitute "sitter" that could be trained both to hatch eggs and to care for chicks. Before the introduction of heated incubators, the most common way to free hens for continued laying while still getting new generations of chickens was to enlist a capon to sit on the nest and tend the young hatchlings. The following instructions for persuading a capon to care for chicks show that love can often be a thorny proposition:

How a Capon May Lead Chickens
[This] he will do naturally, and kindly; and by reason of the largeness of his body, will brood, or cover them easily thirty or forty, he will lead them forth safely, and defend them from Kites, or Buzzards, better than the Hens. The way to make them take charge, is with a fine small bryer [briar], or else sharpe Nettles at night, do

but sting all his breast, and nether parts, and
then in the dark set the Chickens under him; the
warmth or heat taketh away the smart, so he will
fall much in love with them; and whenever he
proveth unkind, you must sting him again, and
this will make him never forsake them.

—Adam Shewring,
The Plain Dealing Poulterer, 1664

Cruel as it seems, the use of nettles was a common
recommendation. Even Oliver Goldsmith, famous
for his celebration of simple virtues in *The Vicar of
Wakefield*, had no qualms about stinging a capon:

Capons may very easily be taught to clutch a
fresh brood of chickens throughout the year; so
that when one little colony is thus reared, another
may be brought to succeed it. Nothing is more
common than to see capons thus employed and
the manner of teaching them is this: first the
capon is made very tame, so as to feed from
one's hand; then about evening, they pluck the
feathers off his breast, and rub the bare skin with
nettles; they then put the chickens to him, which
presently run under his breast and belly and

probably rubbing his bare skin gently with their heads allay the stinging pain which the nettles had just produced. This is repeated for two or three nights, till the animal takes an affection to the chickens that have thus given him relief, and continues to give them the protection they seek for: perhaps also the querulous voice of the chickens may be pleasant to him in misery, and invite him to succour the distressed.

—Oliver Goldsmith, *A History of the Earth and Animate Nature*, 1774

A gentler suggestion comes from France, showing sympathy for the plight of the lonely capon and also implying that a drunken gentleman should always take care of strangers found in his bed.

Excluded from the society of rooster and hens, [the capon] seeks out that of chicks, of which he makes friends. One can even use this tendency to make him hatch eggs.

To ensure his goodwill, make him drunk with a stuffing of grain soaked in brandy; then laying his head under his wing, take him gently with both hands and lift him in the air with a slow rocking motion, until he is fast asleep. Then carefully lay him on a nest prepared in advance and garnished with a few eggs. Upon waking, the contact of the eggs, still warm from the heat he has transferred to them, awakens in him the instinct to nest, as it would in a hen, and he carries out the maternal duty; later he leads the little ones, when they are hatched, like a real mother.

One can make a capon adopt chicks that he did not hatch, by the same process, insinuating them under his wings, one by one, when he is asleep. When he wakes, their contact tears from him little cries of pleasure and it is with the most willing spirit that he takes control of their education.

—*Larousse Encyclopedia of Domestic Life*, 1926

ON BREEDS

My Favorite Chicken

Chickens have traveled so far, lived so long, interbred so enthusiastically, and acquired so many different names across the centuries that it is very difficult to keep track of the different varieties. This has not kept anyone from trying, or from finding other means of classifying birds.

Some early observers ranked chickens by color. In ancient Rome, dark-colored birds were preferred:

It is not expedient to purchase any fowls but the most fruitful: and let them be of a very red, or a dark-coloured feather, with black pinions [The pinion is the outer part of the wing]: and, if it can be done, let them be all chosen of this colour, or of that next to it. If otherwise, let the white be avoided; which, as they are for the most part tender, and not very long-lived, so such of them as are fruitful are not easily found: and, being also very conspicuous, they are, by reason of their remarkable white colour, very frequently snatched away by hawks and eagles.

—Columella, *Of Husbandry*, c. 65 AD

Just before the modern age of "scientific" poultry breeding, Walter Dickson identified eight different varieties of "the barn door fowl," none of which is found in modern poultry charts:

The fowl with a small comb; the crowned fowl; the silver-coloured fowl; the slate-blue fowl; the chamois-coloured fowl; the ermine-like fowl; the widow, which has white tear-like spots on a dark ground; and the fire and stone coloured fowls.

—Walter Dickson, *Poultry*, 1838

As poultry moved into the show ring and prices for exotic species rose to dizzying heights, sometimes reaching several hundred dollars for a single bird, owners began crossing their stock and paying close attention to the hybrid offspring. New breeds like the Rhode Island Red, the Wyandotte, and the Chantecler were introduced, along with many dubious oddities and a large number of exotic eggs whose unwary buyers soon discovered they were hatching ostrich, ducks, and even lizards. The frenzy and fraud surrounding the new breeds prompted some writers to provide *very* specific rules for how to identify a proper specimen:

The [Shanghai] Hen should have a slightly curved *beak* seven-eighths of an inch long, measuring from the tip to the angle of the mouth, and the more yellow this is, the greater the improvement of her countenance; the *forehead* well arched; *comb* low, not more than half an inch high in its highest part, which should be towards the part furthest back,—single, erect, and slightly and evenly toothed; *wattles* small and curved inward; and the *eye* bright and prominent, with an expression tempering the whole of motherly patience and contentment that is met with in no other fowl. The *neck* eight inches long, but appearing shorter from its curved bearing,— nine inches in circumference where it joins the shoulder, and six inches in circumference where it joins the head. The *body*, from the neck to origin of the tail-feathers, should be ten inches long and gently arched. . . . The girth of the body . . . should be twenty inches. . . . The *thigh* six inches long, seven inches in circumference, and densely covered with fluffy feathers. . . . *Middle toe* three and a half inches long.

—The Rev. W. Wingfield and C. W. Johnson, Esq.,
The Poultry Book, 1853

The need for consistent standards for judging poultry shows inspired the exacting requirements still observed today in defining a perfect specimen of every breed. In fact, *The Standard of Perfection*, first published in 1874 by the newly formed American Poultry Association, is the name of the handbook that codifies the

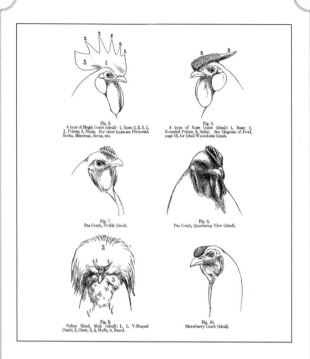

Fig. 5.
A type of Single Comb (ideal): 1, Base; 2, 2, 2, 2, 2, Points; 3, Blade. For other types see Plymouth Rocks, Minorcas, Javas, etc.

Fig. 6.
A type of Rose Comb (ideal): 1, Base; 2, Rounded Points; 3, Spike. See Diagram of Fowl, page 15, for Ideal Wyandotte Comb.

Fig. 7.
Pea Comb, Profile (ideal).

Fig. 8.
Pea Comb, Quartering View (ideal).

Fig. 9.
Sultan Head, Male (ideal): 1, 1, V-Shaped Comb; 2, Crest; 3, 3, Muffs; 4, Beard.

Fig. 10.
Strawberry Comb (ideal).

requirements for different breeds. In 1910, the American Poultry Association divided chicken breeds into Asiatic (Brahmas, Cochins, and Langshans), American (Plymouth Rocks, Dominiques, Wyandottes), and European (Hamburghs, Polands, Dorkings, Spanish, Leghorns, Crevecoeur, Houdan, LaFleche, among many others). The Australorp, an Australian hybrid of the Orpington, had not yet been introduced and neither had the Canadian Chantecler, so the categorization of Commonwealth chickens was left blessedly unexplored. The Rhode Island Red, by the way, was not recognized until after 1910—although it is now the official bird of its namesake state.

Different chickens excel for different purposes, and some authorities classify chickens by their useful traits:

As layers: Leghorns, Hamburghs, Minorcas or Andalusians, Houdans, Langshans, Wyandottes, Spanish, Brahmas, Plymouth Rocks, Polish, Game, Cochins, La Fleche.

La Fleche

For quality of meat: Game, La Fleche, Dorkings, Crevecoeurs, Houdans, Polish, Wyandottes, Langshans, Brahmas.

For size and weight: Brahmas, Cochins, Dorkings, Langshans, Plymouth Rocks, Crevecoeurs, La Fleche, Malays.

For hardiness: Leghorns, Houdans, Wyandottes, Brahmas, Langshans, Cochins, Minorcas, and Andalusians.

As sitters and mothers: Dorkings, Game, Dumpies, Silkies, Brahmas, Cochins.

We might perhaps add that for combination of useful qualities generally we would name Houdans, Plymouth Rocks, Langshans, and Minorcas, as most worth of attention.

—Lewis Wright, *Illustrated Book of Poultry*, 1890

Individual chicken fanciers continued to have firm—and highly varied—opinions about the best breeds.

Shanghaes are the most domestic and amiable of all the varieties of poultry. . . . Yet let no one suppose that they are without becoming high spirit. No cocks come forward more gallantly to repel the trespassing Lothario; and none are

Plymouth Rocks

more generous, in giving precedence to the ladies at feeding times, than are those of the Shanghae.
—Wingfield and Johnson, *The Poultry Book*, 1853

As a table fowl the Dorking is unsurpassed. The meat is fine and abundant, especially on the breast and wings. The hen is a good sitter and mother, but not much of a layer, except when young. . . .

Leghorns are astonishingly good layers, especially the Whites, and the eggs are of good size. They are hardy and precocious, laying and breeding very early. As a table bird they are not notable. . . .

The Wyandotte is a very handsome and hardy bird. They lay well, grow fast, and are a good table fowl—in fact, the ideal fowl for both fancier and farmer.

—*Pratt's Poultry Pointers*, 1901

White Leghorns

The Plymouth Rocks, Light Brahmas and Buff Orpingtons are all good table birds, but the last named breed is by far the choicest, being finer grained and more juicy than the other two.

—Ernest Pryce Mitchell, *A Practical Poultry Plant for Southern California*, 1904

When a fancier of poultry views for the first a good specimen of the Blue Laced Andalusian, we note that he invariably characterizes it as "beautiful," and with good reason, for the combination of color presented is certainly a pleasing one—the red, white and blue of our national emblem—but "handsome is as handsome does," and lovely as they are, the Andalusians' strongest claim to popular favor lies in the direction of utility.

—*Inglenook Poultry Yards*, c. 1905

Sometimes beauty is its own justification.

The Golden Polands, when well-bred, are exceedingly handsome; the Cock having golden hackles, and gold and brown feathers on the back. . . . The Hen is richly laced with dark brown or black on an ochre ground; legs light blue, very cleanly made. . . . The Hens of the Silver Polands are much more ornamental than the Cocks; though even they are sure to attract notice.

—Edmund Saul Dixon,
Ornamental and Domestic Poultry, 1848

Golden Spangled Polands

In the end, the sensitive observer will find beauty in any breed.

Most cocks, even those of the commonest species, being considered, when exposed to the light of the sun, shine with the brightest colours, with the beauty and odd mixture of which we are the more struck as we are most intent in looking at them.

The hens themselves, if we have been mindful of having them of the finest kinds, are adorned in a manner no less worthy to be admired. Some of them have spots distributed with a kind of regularity, and so brightly white that they have

Wyandottes and Plymouth Rocks

been called silvered hens on that account. Others go by the name of gilt hens, because they are deck'd with spots which look like gold when viewed in the sun. The more common colours are distributed with innumerable varieties on the ordinary hens. This class of birds, designed to be for ever under our eyes, offer a multitude of colours, the several shades of which would be very difficultly found, if they were sought for among the birds of the forests, the river and the sea, of a great many species.

—René Antoine Ferchault de Réaumer,
On the Art of Hatching and Bringing Up
Domestic Fowls, 1749

Leghorns and Minorcas

SECRET ARTS

Laying, Hatching, and Preserving Eggs

When chickens first arrived in Egypt, some four thousand years ago, they were called "the bird that lays every day." Few keepers of poultry have found their hens to be quite that productive, particularly in the winter. Only in the 1930s did researchers discover

that putting lights in the henhouse to create a "day" of fourteen hours stimulated egg production. Before then, poultry keepers spent centuries exploring other ways to keep hens laying.

Many early authorities believed hens could be induced to lay eggs year-round if given a special diet.

> On getting hens to lay in winter: ye must nourish them with toasted bread, soked in ale, or small-wine, mixte with some water. Some doe take of water and milke, and soake the toastes therein, from the evening to the morning, and so give it to them on the morrow to their breakfast, and at night they give them oates or barley.
>
> —Leonard Mascall, *The Husbandlye Ordering and Government of Poultrie*, 1581

Fitches, also known as black cumin or nutmeg flower, is the seed of Nigella sativa, mentioned in the Bible and used for flavoring and as a medicine since ancient days.

> If you feed your hens oft with toast taken out of Ale, with Barley boyl'd, or Fitches, they will lay oft and all the Winter.
>
> —Adam Shewring, *The Plain Dealing Poulterer*, 1664

If Fowls are fed with Buck or French-Wheat, or with Hemp-seed, they say, they will lay more Eggs than ordinary.

—J. Mortimer, *The Whole Art of Husbandry*, 1708

S.W. Cole says that hens will never lay well in winter, unless they are made to "scratch for a living." This is done by burying their grain several inches in gravel. He states that eight hens which did not lay an egg in a month in winter, by adopting this course, laid three times as many eggs the following winter, as their whole feed cost.

—*Illustrated Annual Register of Rural Affairs*, 1864

Other authorities insisted you could tell a good layer by its color:

It is important to choose fertile hens, which are indicated by red feathers, black wings, unequal toes, large heads, combs upstanding and heavy, for such hens are most likely to lay.

—Varro, *Country Matters*,
c. 36 BCE

Or its age:

The young hens are more useful for laying than for hatching eggs; and their desire of brooding is checked by passing a small quill through their nostrils.

—Columella, *Of Husbandry*, c. 65 AD

Or possibly its weight, because even a hen may benefit from slimming down:

Very small eggs are often laid regularly by hens so fat internally that there is not room in the egg passage for a normal sized egg to form. The remedies are: *reduced food*, and *exercise*.
—John Henry Robinson, *Poultry-Craft*, 1899

Or maybe the problem is of an impatient owner:

Everyone knows that the first eggs of a hen are small; but people may be ignorant that some hens lay the second, the third, and the fourth year, eggs much bigger than those they afforded during the first year.
—René Anotoine Ferchault de Réaumer, *On the Art of Hatching and Bringing Up Domestic Fowls*, 1749

If a hen needs encouragement to start laying, it helps to make her think she has already begun. The humble nest egg is a very ancient contrivance most often made of wood, stone, pottery, or glass—though old golf balls sometimes serve as a modern substitute.

The Eggs should be taken out of the Nest every Day, and the proper Time is the Afternoon, when every Hen has left them. The Nest Egg is always to be left, but never any more; and in the Place of a Nest Egg, some cut a Lump of Chalk into the Form, and it answers the Purpose.

—Thomas Hale, *A Compleat Body of Husbandry*, 1758

The incubation and hatching of eggs has its own vocabulary. After a hen has laid somewhere between six and ten eggs, known as a *clutch* or *brood*, she may get *broody*, developing a plaintive, inward-looking personality that *brooding* humans share. Then she will stop laying to *set* on the nest and incubate her eggs. Poultry keepers often remove the eggs briefly after eight to twelve days to *candle* them, shining a bright light through the shell to see if the egg shows blood spots or rings that are signs of infection. Even worse is the fatal clearness of the undeveloped egg that Aristotle called a *wind egg*. Bad eggs should not be returned to the nest, because they will eventually break; few people today have ever experienced the malodorous consequences when a bad egg breaks, but the nasty smell of *rotten eggs* is still famous far beyond the henhouse.

Hatching, like laying, has inspired much advice over the centuries. The first necessity is a proper nest:

The usual manner of setting eggs under hens, delivered to us by those who manage these things with greater ceremony and superstition, is such as this:

First, they choose the most retired nests they can find, that the brooding hens may not be

disquieted by other fowls: then they clean them carefully before they put straw unto them, and thoroughly purify the straw they are going to lay under them, with sulphur, bitumen, and a burning torch; and, after they have expiated it, they throw it into their beds, and so make hollow nests for them, lest, when they fly into them, or leap out of them, the eggs be rolled out, and fall down.

Very many people also lay a little grass, or small branches of Laurel, under the straw, in their nests; as also heads of garlick with iron nails: all which things are believed to be remedies or preservatives against thunders, whereby the eggs are spoiled, and the half-formed chickens are destroyed before they are perfected in all their parts.

—Columella, *Of Husbandry*, c. 65 AD

To perfume her Nest with Brimstone is good, but with Rosemary much better.

—Nathan Bailey, *Dictionarium Rusticum &*
Urbanicum: or, A Dictionary of all
Sorts of Country Affairs, 1704

It is taken for granted, the box and nest have been made perfectly clean for the reception of the hen, and that a new nest has not been sluggishly and sluttishly thrown upon an old one.

—Bonington Moubray, Esq., *A Practical Treatise on Breeding, Rearing, and Fattening, All Kinds of Domestic Poultry*, 1824

No matter how lovely and perfumed the nest provided, hens often decide to lay in a hidden spot of their own choosing. Hunting for the nest can be a nuisance, or a lark.

Sometimes it is most difficult to find out where they really are laying—as when they choose a bed of nettles, or the ivy at the top of a high wall. Anyhow, when laying eggs hens exhibit

extraordinary fancies for particular places; and it almost seems as if, for the time being, they *could* not lay except in the place of their choice. If they are debarred from it, they will make the most abnormal efforts to reach it. And yet sometimes the place is so ordinary that one wonders what there is to commend it. But in these cases, as in the case of poets and artists, the operation is too sacred to be interfered with.

—Edward Carpenter and George Merrill, "Animal Speech: The Language of Domestic Fowls," *The Humanitarian,* 1913

One of the keenest pleasures of my boyhood days on that old Indiana farm was hunting eggs. The

boy that has never hunted eggs on a real old farm with barns, and sheds, and straw stacks, and hay fields of timothy and clover has missed a great treat.
—Charles Weeks, *Egg Farming in California*, 1919

One reason hens may hide their nests is so that humans will be kept away long enough for the eggs to hatch, a process that takes approximately twenty-one days. During these three weeks of incubation, the mother hen stays on her eggs except for very short periods to get food or water, rising only to stretch and to rotate the eggs with her feet. Or at least, that is what she is supposed to do. Some hens are better brooders than others, and young hens are particularly apt to forget their responsibilities and wander away from the nest. For this reason, older hens or capons are often pressed into service to hatch the eggs.

In the choice of hens to sit, choose the elder, for they are constant and will sit out their Times; but if to lay, choose the youngest, for they are lusty, and prone to the Act of engendering: But for neither purpose choose a fat Hen; for if you set her, she will forsake her Nest; and to keep her to lay, she will lay her Eggs without Shells; besides

which, she will grow slothful, and neither delight
in the one nor the other Act of Nature.

—Nathan Bailey, *Dictionarium Rusticum &*
Urbanicum: or, A Dictionary of all Sorts of
Country Affairs, 1704

In a pinch, humans can also hatch eggs.

A story is told of a drunkard in Syracuse, how he
used to put eggs into the ground under his rush-mat
and to keep on drinking until he hatched them.

—Aristotle, *The History of Animals*, 350 BCE

Pliny has recorded the success of Livia, in
hatching a chicken in her bosom, an act of
patient curiosity which has been paralleled by
several French ladies, who have, in the same way,
proved themselves the mothers of gold-finches
and canary birds.

—Bonington Moubray, Esq.,
A Practical Treatise on Breeding, Rearing, and
Fattening, All Kinds of Domestic Poultry, 1824

Gas and electric incubators—elegant contraptions
that not only maintain a perfect temperature but also

rotate the eggs on revolving racks—were perfected and marketed extensively by the late nineteenth century. Before that, older hens and capons were cajoled into doing the job. But for centuries, there had been rumors of a secret method used in Egypt:

Eggs are hatched by the incubation of the mother-bird. In some cases, as in Egypt, they are hatched spontaneously in the ground, by being buried in dung heaps.

—Aristotle, *The History of Animals*, 350 BCE

Apart from the generally known fashion for breeding these animals, [the Egyptians] have an artificial means for raising incredible numbers of chicks. They don't let the chickens incubate their eggs themselves, but through an especially ingenious contrivance, which is just as effective as the forces of nature.

—Diodorus Siculus,
Historic Library, c. 49 BCE

For centuries, travelers continued to report on the mysterious methods by which Egyptians who knew the secret could hatch as many as 100,000 eggs at a time, without a hen or even a capon in sight. In the 1740s, René Antoine Ferchault de Réaumur, a French scientist with a passion for natural history and the time and money to pursue his research, took the apparently unprecedented step of trying to figure out what the Egyptians were doing.

Gesner and Aldrovandus have collected the passages of the ancient, and the others of their own time, that have made mention of the manner of hatching chickens by help of dung, but not one of those that mention it says he had himself put it in practice; and I dare affirm that none of them ever had the good fortune of hatching one single chicken that way: I am even apt to think, that none of them ever attempted the trial. They talk, however, as if nothing was plainer, nothing easier than the doing it; it seems according to them that the whole secret consists in burying eggs in a heap of common dung, and in leaving them there for three weeks together, without taking any further care of them.

—René Antoine Ferchault de Réaumer,
On the Art of Hatching and Bringing Up Domestic Fowls, 1749

Réaumer experimented with incubators heated by wood fires, by decomposing dung, by proximity to baking ovens, and a variety of other means. His 1749 treatise, known in English as *On the Art of Hatching and Bringing Up Domestic Fowls*, became an indispensable reference for would-be chicken hatchers for the next 150 years, but the legendary Egyptian ovens continued to mystify and intrigue.

> Modern travelers, who mention the art as practiced in Egypt, are very deficient in their details; but we ought to wonder the less at this when Father Sicard informs us that it is kept a secret even in Egypt, and is only known to the inhabitants of the village of Berme, and a few adjoining places in the Delta, who leave it as an heir-loom to their children, forbidding them to impart it to strangers. When the beginning of autumn, the season most favourable for hatching, approaches, the people of this village disperse themselves over the country, each taking the management of a number of eggs instructed to his care by those acquainted with the art.
>
> —Charles Knight, *Penny Magazine for the Society for the Diffusion of Useful Knowledge*, 1833

The business of egg-hatching is conducted by the Copts, who carry it on in Upper and Lower Egypt and pay a license to the government. A building containing from 12 to 24 ovens is called a *maamal*, and its charge is 150,000 eggs. An official report for 1831 gives for Lower Egypt 105 of these establishments, using 19,000,000 eggs, of which 13,000,000 produce chickens. This saves the valuable time of 1,500,000 hens for three

weeks of inactivity and several succeeding weeks of care and scratching, enabling them to devote their undivided attention to the other duties of maternity, egg-laying and cackling.

—Edward Henry Knight, *Knight's American Mechanical Dictionary*, 1876

Just in case the many schemes for getting hens to lay all winter didn't work, prudent poultry keepers also preserved eggs to tide them over until spring.

The Chinese delicacy known as thousand-year eggs is made by coating an egg in an alkaline paste (usually a mixture of clay with quicklime, ash, salt, or zinc oxide) and letting it cure for several weeks or months. This not only preserves the egg but also turns the yolk dark green and changes the white into a dark brown jelly.

For those who prefer the original colors, here are some other methods for preserving eggs used in the years before refrigeration.

To preserve eggs they should be rubbed with fine Salt or soaked for three or four hours in brine, and then cleaned off or packed in chaff or straw.

—Varro, *Country Matters*, c. 36 BCE

[Eggs] are kept in very good order during the winter, if you cover them over and over with chaff, or corn-straw; and in summer with bran. Some cover them all over first with bruised salt for six hours, and then wash them, and so lay them deep in straw, chaff, or bran, some lay them in a heap of unbroken beans; others in beans that are bruised; some cover them with unbruised salt; others harden them in lukewarm brine.

—Columella, *Of Husbandry*, c. 65 AD

The Preservation of Eggs for their keeping a long Time, is a thing that has employed the Thoughts of many, and a great Number of Methods have been proposed, many of them idle enough, but some useful. They have been laid in Straw and in Bran, but the first keeps them too cold, and the latter too hot. The putting them up in Malt has been found preferable to either of these. But the best Method is by dipping them in fat. . . . The best way of doing this is by melting a Quantity of Fat over the Fire, and dipping the Eggs in it. They will bring away so much as will cover the Shell sufficiently for this useful Purpose.

—Thomas Hale, *A Compleat Body of Husbandry*, 1758

As regards the preservation of eggs perfectly fresh, and with very little trouble, for six or eight months during the year, or from March to December, I would recommend the following, having thoroughly proved it the past season:—
For every two galls. water add three pints salt, one quart newly slacked lime, and a tablespoon of cream of tartar. Let the keg stand in a cool part of the cellar, putting in your eggs from time to time, and brine sufficient to cover them. If they are fresh when put in, they will come out so after any reasonable length of time as fresh and handsome as new laid eggs.

—Joseph Annin, *The Cultivator*, May 1846

Finally, here's a very nice care package for the off-to-college crowd:

One of the articles of store provisions which farmers from the north of Ireland prepare for their sons who attend the Scottish universities in winter, is butter and eggs. A layer of butter, salted in the usual way, is put at the bottom of a firkin [a small cask, about quarter of a barrel] several inches thick, and over this a number of fresh eggs are stuck, which are covered with another similar layer of butter, and this is repeated alternately till the cask is full. Accordingly, as each successive layer of butter is consumed, a fresh quantity of eggs are uncovered and they are usually as fresh and good, as we can answer from having repeatedly eaten them at the breakfast tables of our friends, as if fresh laid.

—Walter B. Dickson, *Poultry*, 1838

The last word belongs to Poor Richard:

An Egg Today is Better Than a Hen Tomorrow.
—Benjamin Franklin, *Poor Richard's Almanac*, 1734

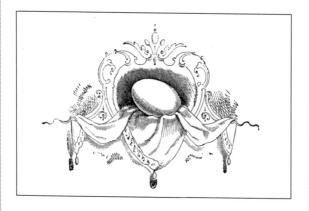

Gold and Silverlaced Bantams

COOPED UP

Building a Palace for Your Poultry

Chickens are homebodies. They go to bed early. They like to crowd together on a perch. Although chickens can and will roost in trees, they much prefer a safer and more comfortable shelter. But where?

The answer depends more on the needs and capacities of the keeper than of the flock. Hen houses can be—and have been—built to just about any style, from chalet to chateau. Queen Victoria had a very large and elegant poultry palace on her grounds at Windsor, stocked with ducks and peacocks as well as chickens; she was so fond of her aviary that she commissioned a painting of the establishment for her personal album. More modest householders could also build henhouses to match their architectural preferences and local materials, from wood to stone to concrete or even fiberglass. Now that chickens are returning to cities, the urban chicken coop business is following, offering modular "Eglus" and modernist pre-fab shelters that advertise "open, loft-like spaces [that] liberate the lifestyles of modern chickens."

In the 1850s, when octagon houses were enjoying a vogue in the United States, poultry journals began offering plans for matching eight-sided chicken coops. But elaborate quarters are not at all necessary, as shown in the practical wisdom of the Sure-Hatch Incubator Company of Clay Center, Nebraska:

> With poultry-raising (like other occupations), the savings go toward making profits. Very often an

organ or piano box will answer every purpose of a home for a small flock of hens. If covered with tar paper, it makes a comfortable and safe small poultry-house.

—Sure Hatch Incubator Company,
Fourth Annual Catalog, c. 1901

Whatever style of coop you like, here are a few good rules that haven't changed much over several millennia:

Choose an enclosed place and there construct two large poultry houses side by side and looking to the East, each about ten by five feet and a little less than five feet in height, and furnished with windows three by four feet in which are fitted shutters of wickerwork, which will serve to let in

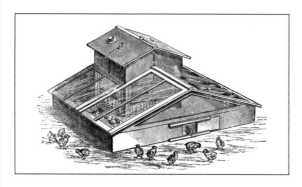

plenty of fresh air and light and yet keep out such vermin as prey upon chickens.

—Varro, *Country Matters*, c. 36 BCE

Now for as much as no Poultry can be kept either in health or safetie abroad, but must of force be housed, you shall understand that your Henne-house would be large and spacious, with somewhat a high roofe, the walls strong, both to keepe out theeves and vermin.

—Gervaise Markham,
Cheape and Good Husbandry, 1614

The House should be placed either near some Kitchen Brew-house, or else some Kiln, where it may have Air of the Fire, and be perfumed with Smoak, which to Pullen is delightful and wholesome.

—Nathan Bailey, *Dictionarium Rusticum &
Urbanicum*, 1704

It is then almost indispensably necessary to prepare a row of lodgings, in number equal to that of the species you have a mind to preserve. These lodgings will be an ornament to your poultry-yard, and will cost but very little, if you will content yourself with making them like those I apply to the same use. A bower of lattice work, thicker wrought than those of gardens, and made like them, either with hoops or with small pantile laths, is the principal and most remarkable part of the edifice. This bower is but five feet high, it is above three feet broad, and its length is determined by that of the ground you have at your disposal. It is divided by means of partitions also of lattice-work, as thick wrought as the rest, into a number of portions, each whereof forms

a lodge. I make the smallest lodges but four feet long, and the biggest but six feet and a half. The least of them is sufficient to harbour a cock with two or three hens, and I put but three or four and a cock into the largest.

—René Antoine Ferchault de Réaumur,
On the Art of Hatching and Bringing Up Domestic Fowls, 1749

The best situation for a poultry-house is facing the east, neither too far nor too near the farm-house. The form may be a parallelogram, of twelve feet long by ten broad, and as many in height. The floor must be raised about a foot above the level of the ground, the walls thick, very rough-cast, white washed without and within, having no chinks, crevices, nor cavities, to harbour polecats, weasels, rats, mice, or even insects.

—Walter B. Dickson, *Poultry*, 1838

Generally speaking a southern exposure is best, east is second choice, west third, and north last or not at all.

—Joseph Tumbach, *How I Made $10,000 in One Year with 4200 Hens*, 1919

Once the building has been designed, questions of landscaping follow:

Whether or not the poultry be suffered to range at large, and particularly to take the benefit of the farm-yard, a separate and well-fenced yard or court must be pitched upon. The foundation should be laid with chalk, or bricklayer's rubbish, the surface to consist of sandy gravel, considerable plots of it being sown with common trefoil, or wild clover, with a mixture of burnet, spurry, or star-grass, which last two species are particularly salubrious to poultry.

—Bonington Moubray, Esq.,
*A Practical Treatise
on Breeding, Rearing, and Fattening,
All Kinds of Domestic Poultry,* 1824

Yards are absolutely unnecessary in getting the greatest profit from fowls, and in fact are a detriment, even if they could be kept free from harmful germs. All poultrymen mean to keep their yards pure, but they never do.

—Charles Weeks, *Egg Farming
in California,* 1919

Perhaps the best thing is to keep the henhouse moving. Here is an early mention of a chicken tractor:

> Mama had a flock of white Leghorn hens in a young orchard, and was selling eggs. According to Bruce, hen houses on runners were moved between the rows of trees where they could be pulled frequently to fresh sites, adding fertilizer to the land. Nests lined each end of the shed-like structures, with roosts stretched in between.
>
> —Dorothy Jenkins Ross, *Life on a Family Fruit Farm in Early California*, 1910

IN SICKNESS AND IN HEALTH

Protecting Chickens Through the Ages

Anyone who keeps chickens soon discovers they get sick. They cough. They wheeze. They freeze. They bloat. They keel over for no discernable reason. People who paid pennies for a baby chick balk at veterinary bills that can reach hundreds of dollars. They may leave the ailing creature to die, or give it to a chicken rescue shelter (yes, such places exist, and they are getting crowded). Those who want to help their chickens may try a home remedy. The cures are almost as various as the complaints, and considerably more colorful.

For many centuries, several respiratory ailments common to chickens were known as the Pip.

Cure for the Pip: There are some who thrust into their gorge cloves of garlick moistened in lukewarm oil. Some wet their mouths with a man's lukewarm urine, and compress them so long, til the fatness of the urine forces them to press out the nauseous phlegm through their nostrils. The berry also, which the Greeks call wild grape, mixed with their meat, is of great benefit to them; or the same bruised, and given them with water for their drink.

—Columella, *Of Husbandry*, c. 65 AD

For the Diseases of Hens eyes: You shall cure a Hens eyes with Womans Milk, or with the juyce of Purslane, anointing their eyes on the outside. Or else anoint them with Ammoniacum and Cummin, and Honey mingled in equall parts together, but bring your Hens into shady places.

For lice in Hens: You shall free Hens from the lowsy disease, with rosted Cummin, and Stavesacre beaten, of each a like quantity, anoint the Hens with these mingled with Wine: also you may wash them with the decoction of wild Lupins.

—Johann Jacob Wecker, *Eighteen Books of the Secrets of Art & Nature*, 1582

Andreas Cesalpinus writes that the inner bark of the ash tree, which makes the water in which it has been steeped blue in color, should be given to hens when they are afflicted with diseases, but he does not say which diseases or on whose authority he recommends this.

—Ulisse Aldrovandi, *Ornithology*, 1599

The fluxe in Poultrie commeth with eating too much moyst meate. The cure is, to give them Pease-branne scaled, and it will stay them.

—Gervaise Markham,
Cheape and Good Husbandry, 1614

For grown fowls affected by the roup, warm lodging is necessary, and even the indulgence of the fire, or the warmth of the bake-house. Wash the nostrils with warm soap and water, as often as necessary, and the swollen eyes with warm milk and water. Afterwards bathe the swollen parts with camphorated spirits, or brandy and warm water. As a finish to the cure, give sulphur in the

drink, or a small pinch of calomel in dough, three times in a week.

—Bonington Moubray, Esq.
A Practical Treatise on Breeding,
Rearing, and Fattening, All Kinds of
Domestic Poultry, 1824

When time is available for individual treatment a bird with a cold can be cured quickly. A teaspoonful of castor oil; a careful cleansing of the nostrils . . . with a soft cloth; the injection into each nostril and the cleft of the mouth of a minute quantity of kerosene, by means of a little "squirt" oil can, milk-moistened mash for a few days, or bread and milk—these measures will result in a quick and complete recovery.

—Joseph Tumbach, *How I Made $10,000 in*
One Year with 4200 Hens, 1919

Some treatments seem dauntingly complex, dangerous, and also very possibly illegal. The following cure for chicken cholera includes laudanum, a mixture of opium dissolved in alcohol that was a popular nineteenth-century cure-all for man and beast alike.

Don't
Worry!

Conkey
Will Cure
Me.

COPYRIGHT 1908

CONKEY'S POULTRY REMEDIES

Chicken Cholera.—If diagnosed at an early stage recovery may be expected in nearly half of the cases from the administration every three hours of:

Rhubarb...5 grains

Cayenne Pepper...2 grains

Laudanum...10 drops

Administering midway between each dose a tea-spoonful of brandy diluted with rather less than its bulk of water, into which have been dropped five drops of M'Dugall's Fluid Carbolate, or three grains of salicine.

—Lewis Wright, *Illustrated Book of Poultry*, 1890

Sometimes, though, the cure is simplicity itself:

A fowl will sometimes all of a sudden run round in a circle, or stagger about as if drunk, from congestion or some other pressure on the brain. The immediate remedy is to hold its head for a good while under a stream of water, such as a water-tap.

—Lewis Wright, *Illustrated Book of Poultry*, 1890

Chickens face many dangers besides disease, as shown by the following cautions and cures.

If it thunders while a hen-bird is brooding, the eggs get addled.

—Aristotle, *The History of Animals*, 350 BCE

Deer's horn should be burnt around their coops to keep snakes away, for the very smell of those vermin is fatal to young chickens.

—Varro, *Country Matters*, c. 36 BCE

Either a diligent old woman, or a boy, [should] be appointed to keep [chickens], and watch over them when they wander up and down, lest they be snatched away, either by men who lay wait for them, or be taken in the snares of insidious animals.

—Columella, *Of Husbandry*, c. 65 AD

The threat of foxes, cats, snakes, and even insects inspires extreme measures.

Foxes do not attack roosters who have eaten the dry liver of that animal or if the roosters wear a skin taken from a fox around their neck.

—Pliny, *Natural History*, 79 AD

Some say that a Fox boyled and cut into pieces, and given to Hens for meat, will defend the Hens from all Foxes for two Moneths. . . . This was tried in the Valley of Angus called Glenmores, in Scotland, where there are great store of Foxes.

A Cat will never come near a Hen, if you hang under the Hens Wing wild Rue; nor will a Fox or any other Creature hurt them.

—Johann Jacob Wecker, *Eighteen Books of the Secrets of Art & Nature*, 1582

Of Poultery being Stung: If they be stung with any venomous Worms, or venomous thing, as you may perceive by their lowring and swelling; if so, then you must anoint them with Rue and Butter mixt together and it helpeth.

—Adam Shewring, *The Plain Dealing Poulterer*, 1664

Sometimes it seems you can't do anything right:

It is well known that much cold renders fowls torpid, retards and diminishes their laying; that much heat enfeebles them; that the want of good water brings on many disorders; that too much moisture induces rheumatic swellings; and that an infected atmosphere makes them sickly, less prolific, injures their flesh, and makes them difficult to rear. From these circumstances may be deduced the principles upon which the poultry-yard should be regulated.

—Walter B. Dickson, *Poultry*, 1838

Mineral poisons and nicotine fed to hens in a reckless or ignorant way will so weaken the nervous system and egg organs that a Leghorn hen will lay soft shelled eggs. Don't get me wrong. I am strong for the Leghorn, but you can't treat her like a deaf baby elephant.

—Old Ironspoon,
Petaluma Poultry Journal, 1922

Sometimes all you need is faith and love. And perhaps a bit of poetry. Eccentric poet Nancy Luce lived alone on her farm on Martha's Vineyard, an island off the coast of Massachusetts, where she found great inspiration and companionship in her bantam chickens. Although the following stanza has a mournful tone, it is in fact a tale of miraculous recovery.

POOR LITTLE TWEEDLE TEDEL BEBBEE

When poor little heart Pinky,

Was about six weeks old,

She was taken with the chicken distemper,

Chickens died off all over this island.

She was catching grasshoppers, and crickets,

In the forenoon smart,

At twelve o'clock she was taken sick,

And grew worse.

At one o'clock she was past opening her eyes,

And could not stand,

Her body felt cold

And stiff in my hand.

I give her a portion of Epsom salts,

With a little black pepper in it,

I wept over her that afternoon,

I prayed to the Lord to save me her life.

I sat up that night,

With her in my lap,

Till eleven o'clock that night,

Then she seemed to be better.

Then I put her in a thing, a good soft bed,

And lay down and spoke to her often,

Say how do you do, little dear, she answered me quick,

Then I knew she was better.

The next day I gave her
Warm water to drink,
The third day she was herself,
Got well and smart.
She remained well four years,
And laid me pretty eggs,
Then the Lord thought best to take her from the evil to come,
Without being sick but a very little while.

—Nancy Luce, *A Complete Edition of the Works of Nancy Luce*, 1871

Silver Spangled Hamburghs

COUNT YOUR CHICKENS

The Numerology of Flock and Nest

How many chickens to keep? What is the best proportion of roosters to hens? How many eggs can a hen hatch? How much space does a chicken need? The numerology of poultry is rich, complicated, and hotly contested.

> Two hundred heads are a sufficient number for employing the whole care of one person to feed them.
>
> —Columella, *Of Husbandry*, c. 65 AD

> The best eastern poultry journals fix the profitable limit at two thousand birds, and the repeated failures of plants that have started on a much larger scale seem to bear them out.
>
> —Ernest Pryce Mitchell,
> *A Practical Poultry Plant for Southern California*, 1904

> The number of hens that can be kept on a given space is a question involving many problems. . . .

In attempting to answer it we must first of all agree that we will give the hens yards; the writer cannot hazard an opinion otherwise as he does not favor the no-yard idea. On this basis it is reasonable to count on 1000 hens to the acre with a minimum of 5 acres, or about 800 to the acre with a minimum of 2½ or 3 acres.

—Joseph H. Tumbach,
*How I Made $10,000 in One Year with
4200 Hens*, 1919

And what is the proper ratio of roosters and hens?

Provide five females each.

—Columella, *Of Husbandry*, c. 65 AD

A correspondent in France informed me, that my little book had reached that country so celebrated for poultry, and that the good housewives of France made themselves very merry with my practice of restricting the cock to so few as half a dozen hens, their allowance being twenty, or even twenty-five. . . . What difference, in such respect, may subsist between the soil or animals of England and France, I am not qualified to determine; I can only assure the reader that my rule is the result of long and actual experience.

—Bonington Moubray, Esq., *A Practical Treatise on Breeding, Rearing, and Fattening, All Kinds of Domestic Poultry*, 1824

How Many Hens to a Male? The general rule is:—for Asiatics, 6 to 10; for Americans, 8 to 12; for Mediterraneans [sic], 10 to 15.

—John Henry Robinson, *Poultry-Craft*, 1899

Chicken fanciers, like fishermen, may be tempted to exaggerate, particularly when describing egg production. How many eggs can a hen really lay without the help of artificial lights, growth hormones, and other industrial inducements?

What is a Good Egg Yield? There are ordinary, *extraordinary*, and very extraordinary egg yields. An ordinary egg yield is from six to ten dozen eggs per hen per year. An extraordinary yield is from ten to fourteen dozen per hen. Anything over fourteen dozen eggs per hen is a very extraordinary egg yield.

—John Henry Robinson, *Poultry-Craft*, 1899

Many people talk of the two hundred egg a year hen as though she were an established fact. I find that a hundred and thirty-two eggs a year, is a good average to work on. . . . I would not knowingly hatch eggs from a two hundred egg hen towards the end of the season, for the progeny would naturally be weaklings. The tremendous drain on the vitality of the hen would, in my opinion, finish her in a season as a breeder.

—Ernest Pryce Mitchell, *A Practical Poultry Plant for Southern California,* 1904

As for the best number of eggs for a setting hen, the only thing experts seem to agree on is that an uneven number is highly desirable. Ulisse Aldrovandi, the first professor of natural history at the very ancient University of Bologna, published his *Ornithology* in 1599. Much of the text concerns what even earlier authors had to say on the subject of chickens:

Almost all of those who have written on agriculture urge that an unequal number be placed under the hen; at the present day I do not know how carefully our farm girls observe this rule. For in actual fact it does not seem to lack superstition unless we happen to regard the thoughts of Pythagoras as wise: he placed the greatest good in an unequal number. . . . If the hen is fertile Florentinus insists not more than twenty-three eggs should be placed under her, but fewer eggs when she is not fertile. Varro and Pliny say she should not incubate more than twenty-five eggs even though because of her fertility she has laid more. Columella wishes no more than fifteen to be placed under her in the first breeding season, in the month of January; nineteen in March, no fewer; and twenty-one in April and the entire summer up to the first of October. But our women almost always show the chickens no more than seventeen or nineteen for hatching.

—Ulisse Aldrovandi, *Ornithology*, 1599

Or, to put it more briefly,

As to the Number of Eggs to be put under a Hen for setting, there have been different Opinions; but by what I have found from many Trials, the best Number is seventeen.

—Thomas Hale, *A Compleat Body of Husbandry*, 1758

White Cochins

DUMB CLUCKS AND BIRDBRAINS

Can a Chicken Beat You at Checkers?

Despite the persistence of insults like "dumb cluck," there is growing scientific evidence that chickens are hardly birdbrains. In 2009, animal psychologists showed that newly hatched chicks were able to do simple arithmetic and understand that objects still exist even when moved out of sight—a level of wisdom it takes human children quite a bit longer to acquire. Gambling casinos in the United States have started offering "man vs. chicken" events in which the challenge is a game of tic-tac-toe and the stars are trained chickens that take turns against human opponents, working in a glass enclosure where they peck a special board to indicate their next move. The chickens win more often than not—so often, in fact, that the games are presented as entertainment and betting is not allowed. But scientific fascination with chicken intelligence goes back much farther.

> The rooster's is a natural intelligence which does not arise from deliberate thought itself.
>
> —Ulisse Aldrovandi, *Ornithology*, 1599

Many creatures are endowed with a ready discernment to see what will turn to their own advantage and emolument; and often discover more sagacity than could be expected. Thus my neighbour's poultry watch for wagons loaded with wheat, and running after them pick up a number of grains which are shaken from the sheaves by the agitation of the carriages.

—Gilbert White,
The Natural History of Selborne, 1789

Charles Darwin was impressed by the cognitive abilities of a mother hen:

I may quote the following case in which a fowl adopted the habit of conveying, not her eggs, but her young chickens. I quote it from Houzeau . . . who gives the observation on the authority of his brother as eyewitness. The fowl had found good feeding-ground on the further side of a stream four metres wide. She adopted the habit of flying across with her chickens upon her back, taking one chicken on each journey. She thus transferred her whole brood every morning, and brought them back in a similar way to their nest every evening. The habit of carrying young in this way is not natural to Gallinaceæ, and therefore this particular instance of its display can only be set down as an intelligent adjustment by a particular bird.

—Charles Darwin, *Notebooks*, undated entry

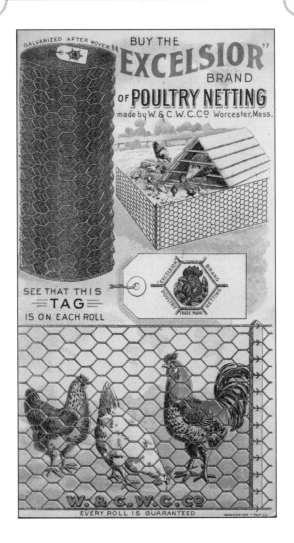

Other observers fear that domestication has harmed the chicken's natural wit:

There is a good deal to show that the sureness and precision of their instincts have, in the case of domestic fowls, been adversely affected by their long dependence on man. . . . Fowls on the outside of a large pen, when they see the others being fed inside, will almost invariably rush violently against the wire-netting in vain endeavour to reach the food—though they have been round hundreds of times by the usual entrance, and must know it perfectly well; and it is only occasionally that some exceptional genius, after a few efforts at the netting, bethinks herself of the better way.

—Edward Carpenter and George Merrill, "Animal Speech: The Language of Domestic Fowls," *The Humanitarian*, 1913

While the debate over chicken intelligence continues, there is no question that they are a chatty bunch.

No inhabitants of a yard seem possessed of such a variety of expression and so copious a language as common poultry. Take a chicken of four or five days old, and hold it up to a window where there are flies and it will immediately seize its prey, with little twitterings of complacency, but if you tender it a wasp or a bee, at once its note becomes harsh and expressive of disapprobation and a sense of danger. When a pullet is ready to lay, she intimates the event by a joyous and easy soft note. Of all the occurrence of their life that of laying seems to be the most important; for no sooner has a hen disburthened herself, than she rushes forth with a clamorous kind of joy, which the cock and the rest of his mistresses immediately adopt. The tumult is not confined to the family concerned, but catches

from yard to yard, and spreads to every homestead within hearing, till at last the whole village is in an uproar. As soon as a hen becomes a mother, her new relation demands a new language; she then runs clocking and screaming about, and seems agitated as if possessed. The father of the flock has also a considerable vocabulary: if he finds food, he calls a favourite concubine to partake; and if a bird of prey passes over, with a warning voice he bids his family beware. The gallant chanticleer has, at command, his amorous phrases and his terms of defiance. But the sound by which he is best known is his crowing: by this he has been distinguished in all ages as the countryman's clock or larum, as the watchman that proclaims the divisions of the night.

—Gilbert White, *The Natural History of Selborne*, 1789

Mark Twain agreed chickens were intelligent conversationalists, although he wasn't positive about the message:

"Dumb" beast suggests an animal that has no thought-machinery, no understanding, no speech, no way of communicating what is in its mind. We know that a hen *has* speech. We cannot understand every thing she says, but we easily learn two or three of her phrases. We know when she is saying "I have laid an egg"; we know when she is saying to the chicks, "Run here, dears, I've found a worm"; we know what she is saying when she voices a warning: "Quick! Hurry! Gather yourselves under mamma, there's a hawk coming!" . . . The clearness and exactness of the few of the hen's speeches which we understand are argument that she can communicate to her kind a hundred things which we cannot comprehend—in a word, that she can converse.

—Mark Twain, *What is Man?*, 1905

In recent years, scientists working in laboratories under rigorously controlled conditions have discovered that chickens have multiple "food calls," "alarm calls," and "contact calls," which is a formal name for all the ways the birds say hello. But in 1913, long before animal psychology became an academic field, a pair of political activists living in the English countryside put together a glossary of chicken-speak that has only been confirmed by later research. Here is their twenty-three word dictionary:

Hens

1. Cry of Alarm: at hawk or any large bird overhead—a shrill squeal, and in general run for shelter; but see number 11.

2. Cry of Alarm: at animal on the ground, e.g. a rat; a hasty, disorganised cackle, somewhat like number 5, but different. Less anxious and terrified than number 1.

3. Cry (hysteric): when chased by another hen—a sort of "ha, ha, ha, ha, ha."

4. Prating.—This is a curious creaking sound, like a rusty door, kept up in a continuous way—a sort of complaining and talking to

oneself. The country folk call it "prating." Often used by hens before laying; also when they are waiting for food.

5. Cackling proper.—This is the well-known note after laying. It has a tendency to fly up in the musical interval of a sixth, or an augmented sixth. And somehow the latter interval seems to be peculiarly appropriate. The resolution of the chord of the augmented sixth on the common chord of the key is just what the hen must feel in laying an egg. Sometimes, however (we suppose by force of association), the cackle is used before laying.

6. Grumbling.—as when gently lifted off their nests; a soft, rumbling, almost good-humoured sound.

7. Scolding.—A harsh grating sound, as when their chicks are interfered with.

8. Clucking or Clocking.—A musical bell-like sound, used as call to food for chicks.

9. The same, but less definite and more irregular; used when breaking up food for the chicks. (N.B.—It is curious and interesting that, when going "broody," hens will use both 8 and 9. It is as if the image of the wished for chicks was in their mind, and called up the note.)

10. Warning, not to eat, used for chicks: a short grating sound. Commonly used by hens when any unknown substance is thrown down for food; and instantly obeyed by the chicks—until the mother, having tried the substance, gives them permission by number 8.

11. Warning to chicks of danger: a short dry cluck—and when a bird is overhead, the mother squats down as signal to chicks to do the same—who then remain motionless, but with their eyes wide open.

12. A sullen short cluck, related to number 11; used as a signal to chicks to follow.

13. Crooning: used by the hen when her chicks are gathering under her.

14. Purring: a different sound, used when all are settled down.

15. A low coo: a mark of favour towards the cock bird, when being courted by him.

16. A whining cry of remonstrance, when objecting to these attentions.

17. Crowing, something like the cock, but not, of course, so effectually. This is often used by old hens, when past breeding; and sometimes by young ones having other male characteristics like well-marked combs and tail feathers.

Notes of Cock-Birds

18. Crowing.—This seems to be originally of the nature of a challenge. As far as we have observed, the note when challenging a rival to fight is the same as the usual morning call. The crow is evidently an expression of pride and strength, and so also of reassurance to the hens.

19. Call to food for hens.—A cluck, cluck, but somewhat different from that of the hens.

20. Cackling, when a hen cackles. This is apparently done out of sympathy; but it is a rougher, ruder sound than the cackle of the hen, and can easily be distinguished from it.

21. Cooing, when making love; but stronger than the coo of the hen, and sometimes compared to a neigh.

22. When on the perch at night, and all settled down, the cock gives a long low sound. There is also

23. A low warning sound, given by the cock when there is any disturbance at night, and taken up by the hens.

—Edward Carpenter and George Merrill,
"Animal Speech: The Language of
Domestic Fowls," *The Humanitarian*, 1913

Wyandottes

WHEN IN DOUBT, ASK A CHICKEN
Poultry for Seekers and Believers

Chicken Little, hit on the head by an acorn, became convinced that the sky was falling; he (or is it she?) is the model of the foolish pessimist. But not all fears are misplaced, and many people have concluded they should pay attention to any message the chicken brings.

In ancient Rome, it was widely held that the success of an enterprise could be predicted by the behavior of certain chickens. Sacred birds were brought from the Island of Negroponte and guarded by special priests, called Pullarii, who could foretell events by watching how the chickens ate or drank. In 249 BC, during the first Punic War, the Roman general Publius Claudius should have been forewarned of his defeat at the Battle of Drepana when the sacred chickens on his ship refused to feed before the battle. Disregarding the omen, Claudius threw the chickens overboard, with the grim quip, "Ut biberent, quando essen nollent" (Let them drink, since they won't eat). After his defeat, the general was called back to Rome and fined for impiety and incompetence.

Classical authors tried to predict the sex of a chicken from the shape of its egg.

> Long and pointed eggs are female; those that are round, or more rounded at the narrow end, are male.
>> —Aristotle, *The History of Animals*, c. 350 BCE

> The rounder Eggs produce Hens, the others yield Cocks.
>> —Pliny, *Natural History*, 79 AD

The Romans also believed that, at least on very rare occasions, chickens might deign to converse with humans:

> We find in our Annals, that in the Territory of Ariminum, when Marcus Lepidus and Quintus Catulus were Consuls, a Dung-hill Cock spoke; and it was at the Villa of Galerious. But this only happened once, so far as I can learn.
>> —Pliny, *Natural History*, 79 AD

Even in silence, chickens are significant omens, for good or ill:

Interpreters of dreams declare that the man who has seen in a dream a flock of hens coming to him and entering his house will be enriched with wealth and honors, but they also add that if little hens have merely been sighted in a dream, they presage a slender amount of these things.

—Ulisse Aldrovandi, *Ornithology*, 1599

Chickens figure in the rituals of many different religions. In the *Hadith*, Muhammad instructs his followers to ask for Allah's blessings when they hear a cock crow, because it means the bird has seen an angel. In the days before the solemn holiday of Yom Kippur, the Day of Atonement, Orthodox Jews twirl chickens around their heads (roosters for men, hens for women), then have the birds killed and donated to the poor. In Indonesia, chickens are an important element of Hindu cremation ceremonies, where they are tethered near the body to absorb the evil spirits that might otherwise attach themselves to living members of the family of the deceased. In Christianity, eggs are closely associated with the celebration of Easter.

In 1533, a bishop of Paris, authorized by a bull from the Pope Julius III, being disposed to permit the use of eggs during Lent, the parliament took offence, and prevented the execution of the Episcopal mandate. It is this severe abstinence from eggs during Lent which gave rise to the custom of having a great number of them blessed on Easter even, to be distributed among friends on Easter Sunday; whence comes the expression, "to give Easter eggs." Pyramids of them were carried into the king's cabinet after the high mass. They were gilded, or admirably painted, and the prince made presents of them to his courtiers.

—Alexis Soyer, *The Pantropheon, or History of Food and Its Preparation from the Earliest Ages of the World*, 1853

The symbol of rebirth can also serve to show the absurdity of theological strife. When Jonathan Swift wanted to satirize the savage futility of religious disputes, he described the warfare between two kingdoms that could not agree on which end to break an egg:

It is allowed on all hands, that the primitive way of breaking eggs, before we eat them, was upon the larger end; but his present majesty's grandfather, while he was a boy, going to eat an egg, and breaking it according to the ancient practice, happened to cut one of his fingers. Whereupon the emperor his father published an edict, commanding all his subjects, upon great penalties, to break the smaller end of their eggs. The people so highly resented this law, that our histories tell us, there have been six rebellions raised on that account; wherein one emperor lost his life, and another his crown. . . . It is computed that eleven thousand persons have at several times suffered death, rather than submit to break their eggs at the smaller end.

—Jonathan Swift, *Gulliver's Travels*, 1726

Long before guinea pigs or mice could be ordered from laboratory supply companies, early scientists used the ever-present chicken for experiments. Athanasius Kircher, a contemporary of Galileo, studied the ways the mind can be fooled by lights, shadows, optical illusions, and the vast power of imagination—including the imagination of a lowly barnyard bird. What follows is the first recorded description of how to hypnotize a chicken.

Experiment 3: On the Radiant Power of Imagination and a Chicken

Tie a chicken by its feet and place it on a floor or pavement. When it first senses that it is captive, it will struggle by every means to shake off its chains, fluttering its wings and moving its whole body. But at last, when its attempt to escape has proven futile, it will calm down as if in despair and place itself at its conqueror's disposal. While the chicken thus remains quiet, draw a line straight forward from its eye with chalk, or any other colored material, on the floor, imitating the shape of the string. Then free the chicken. I tell you that the hen, although it is freed from bondage, will not fly away, even if you urge it to fly. The reason for this is nothing else but the animal's powerful imagination, which takes that line drawn on the floor to be the string by which it is bound. I have often performed this experiment to the amazement of bystanders. Hence there is no doubt that the same phenomenon might have a place in other animals.

—Athanasius Kircher, *The Great Art of Light and Shadow*, 1646

Silkies

Brown Leghorns

THE CHICKEN AS MUSE

Poultry for Poets and Philosophers

The rapt attention a chicken gives to a snail, a worm, a butterfly, or even a stone, can be an inspiring model of close observation for the artist and student of the natural world. There's no need to retreat to a hermitage or cloister when a hen can be your model for the contemplative life.

The man is happy who has an inborn taste for soft and quiet amusements which he may resort to at any time of day: he is still happier when he has good ground to expect from the said amusements curious branches of knowledge, that may become of use to mankind. These may indeed—very properly be called philosophical amusements. The birds of a poultry-yard will afford diversions of this kind to any that shall be fond enough of seeing and observing them.

—René Antoine Ferchault de Réaumer,
*On the Art of Hatching and Bringing Up
Domestic Fowls*, 1749

IMPROVED EXCELSIOR INCUBATOR

I am convinced that Harlequin coming out of an egg upon the stage, is not more astonishing to a child, than the hatching of a chicken both would be, and ought to be, to a philosopher.

—William Paley, *Natural Theology*, 1802

In the early years of the twentieth century, chicken farming was considered a particularly healthful occupation that would rebuild both body and spirit. In 1900, before he became famous as a poet, Robert Frost was instructed by his doctor to find outdoor work. A city boy with no experience of rural life, Frost moved his family to New Hampshire, where he started raising Wyandottes. The effect on his health is uncertain (country air was a plus, terrible hay fever was not), but ten years among poultrymen gave Frost a new vocabulary and a treasury of stories and images he used for the rest of his life. Poems like *A Blue Ribbon at Amesbury,* about a prize-winning hen and a farmer who grapples with cosmic ambitions, reveal how easily the contemplation of chickens can lead one to larger issues. The healthful and morally uplifting qualities of chicken raising were equally clear to many authors who never quite achieved Frost's fame.

A little plot of ground, a little poultry house, a little flock of hens, and a little love for domestic animals, make a combination which will give the poor man in a city, at trifling cost, luxuries for which his rich neighbor is glad to pay liberally.

—John Henry Robinson, *Poultry-Craft*, 1899

Blessed is the man whose choicest pleasure is his work. And how much more satisfactory is that work when we realize that it gives all that this world has to give, health of body and peace of mind and room to exercise all our faculties. . . . To the man who loves animal and plant life, who revels in the sunshine out under the open sky, who is intoxicated with the fresh air and the vigor of an outdoor life, to this man the poultry business is an ideal business.

—Charles Weeks, *Egg Farming in California*, 1919

In a properly ordered world (one where artists need not starve), there should be no conflict between aesthetic and economic benefits:

The care of poultry is to boys and girls a pleasing and profitable work both morally and financially.

The most beautiful breeds make excellent pets and the ownership of something of this nature entirely his own and from which a revenue may be derived impresses young people with the sense of responsibility and inculcates humane ideas, cultivates a business instinct and occupies time that might otherwise be devoted to less inspiring and educational thoughts.

—*American Poultry Journal*, 1900

Andalusians

FINE-FEATHERED FRIENDS

Chickens as Pets

Cuddlier than a calf, less expensive than a horse, doesn't need to be walked, even lays eggs: no wonder chickens often become beloved family pets. Observation leads to admiration, admiration leads to affection, and affection leads to chickens in the house.

> Some years ago, I kept at my country-seat a Hen, which, besides keeping by herself all day long, and wandering about the house apart from the companionship of her fellows, in the evening would go to rest nowhere but close to me among my books, and those rather big ones, although she was often driven away.
>
> —Ulisse Aldrovandi, *Ornithology*, 1599

My earliest recollections are of the hens my mother kept on the old farm in Indiana. Well do I remember the medley of colors and varieties in our flock of barnyard fowl. I played among them and always had my pets. I call to mind one old black hen that to my childish mind seemed almost human. My childish fancy made me a chicken and I played chicken until the hens themselves looked upon me as one of them. How often have I made a nest and sat on it like biddy until my youthful patience was exhausted. Why, I even could understand hen language and talk to them with as much understanding as they could talk to each other. When I clucked the whole flock would come running for the dainty morsel without hesitation. Hen nature is very interesting to a boy and well I knew all the moods and habits of biddy.

—Charles Weeks, *Egg Farming
in California*, 1919

Bantams, the smallest chickens, have long been favorite pets. For centuries, authorities have scoffed at the preference, even while succumbing themselves to the bantam's miniature charms.

I do not too much approve of dwarf fowls; neither on account of their fruitfulness, nor for any other advantage they may bring, unless their very low stature is pleasing to any one.

—Columella, *Of Husbandry*, c. 65 AD

One may come to find at last, that it would be more profitable to bring up hens of that dwarfish kind, which are so very pretty, and whose limbs are all of them so well proportioned, than other hens of a larger species, if any experiment should teach us that the dwarf-hens cost less in proportion in keeping.

—René Antoine Ferchault de Réaumer,
On the Art of Hatching and Bringing Up
Domestic Fowls, 1749

Japanese Bantams

Bantams exist in great variety, and are artificial birds entirely. Their beauty is their chief value. They are useful, however, in the garden, to keep down slugs and insects.

—*Pratt's Poultry Pointers*, 1901

Thomas Jefferson relied on the cuteness of bantam chicks to sweeten the pursuit of natural history, as shown in the following exchange of letters with his granddaughter, who had just turned ten when the letters began:

Thomas Jefferson to Ellen Wayles Randolph (Coolidge), November 30, 1806:

By Davy I send you a pair of Bantam fowls; quite young: so that I am in hopes you will now be

Bantams of Several Varieties

enabled to raise some. I propose on their subject a question of natural history for your enquiry: that is whether this is the Gallina Adrianica, or Adria, the Adsatck cock of Aristotle? For this you must examine Buffon etc.

Ellen Wayles Randolph (Coolidge) to Thomas Jefferson, February 17, 1807:

As for the Bantam she laid one egg in the cold weather and eat it up. I am very much afraid she will do all the others so. If she does she will be as worthless as the others but in spite of that I am very fond of them and think

them very handsome. The old ones are quite tame but the new much to the contrary.

Ellen Wayles Randolph (Coolidge) to Thomas Jefferson, November 11, 1807:

> One of my poor little Bantams is dead and the one which I liked the best although it was the old one. He had got so tame that he could fly up in my lap and eat out of my hand. All the children were sorry at his death.

> —*Family Letters of Thomas Jefferson,*
> ed. Edwin M. Betts and James A. Bear, Jr.

Many affectionate chicken keepers have given names to their birds, but few can rival those that poet Nancy Luce bestowed on her beloved bantam hens: Teedie Lete, Letoogie Tickling, Reanty Fyfante, Pondy Lily, Tealsay Mebloomie, Appe Kaleanyo, Aterryryree Roseendy, Phebea Peadeo, Jaatie Jafy, Speackekey Lepurlyo, Kalallyphe Roseiekey, Levendy Ludandy, Meleany Teatolly, and Vailatee Pinkoatie, among others.

Tweedle Tedel Bebbee Pinky was Luce's favorite, and the feeling seems to have been mutual, as shown in this portrait of bantam devotion:

POOR LITTLE HEART

. . .

From over sea, she was brought to me, one week old,

I raised her in my lap,

She loved me dreadful dearly.

She would jam close to me,

Every chance she could get,

And talk to me, and want to get in my lap,

And set down close.

And when she was out from me,

If I only spoke her name,

She would be sure to run to me quick,

Without wanting anything to eat.

—Nancy Luce, *A Complete Edition of the*
Works of Nancy Luce, 1875

Hamburghs

Houdans

RULES OF THE ROOST
Chickens and the Law

Backyard chickens—scourge or salvation? Most legal restrictions on keeping chickens at home date from the twentieth century. The poultry craze of the 1920s, when popular handbooks suggested that everyone could make money putting hundreds of hens in his yard, led to a backlash of protective zoning. So did the suburban boom of the 1950s, when farmland was being converted into residential communities whose developers wanted to make sure no actual livestock would be slipped in amid the newly built "ranch" houses.

But laws and legal arguments about chickens predate any concerns about noise, smells, or social status. In ancient Rome, where the rich dined in extraordinary opulence and hosts competed for the most excessive feasts, it was the custom to force-feed chickens to make them unnaturally fat and tender. Or at least it was the custom until the legislation described by Pliny the Elder below, which dates from 160 BCE.

Among the old Statutes ordained to repress inordinate Suppers, I find in one Law made by C.

Fannius, the Consul eleven Years before the third Punic War, That no Man should place (on his Table) more than one Hen, which should not be fattened; which Head or Injunction was afterwards taken from this and inserted in all the other Laws.

—Pliny, *Natural History*, 79 AD

Benjamin Franklin, sent to France to promote the "natural rights" of the American colonists, turned the same rhetoric to a facetious argument that it was the law of nature for chickens to be eaten. The following extract is from a mock-legal document sent to a close friend in Paris who had banished her cats for the crime of raiding the henhouse.

Crèvecoeurs

An Humble Petition, Presented to Madame Helvetius by her Cats

...We will ask, in the first place, were the chickens numbered and consigned to our care, and are we answerable for them? Surrounded by so many destructive beings, by mankind in particular, who are firmly persuaded that chickens were only created to be eaten by them, is it on us that the first suspicion can with justice fall? . . . After all, Madam, without wishing to become the apologists of chicken-stealers, let us be permitted to observe, that whatever may be the causes which occasion the diminution complained of in your stock of poultry, they are in the order of nature, and produce a salutary effect to yourself, since they restrain within due bounds the multiplication of this species, which, if suffered to go on unrestrained, would soon convert your whole house into a receptacle for chickens, and reduce you to going without a shift, that no limits may be placed to the number of your fowls.

—Benjamin Franklin, c. 1779 from
The Works of Benjamin Franklin,
ed. Jared Sparks, 1836

Common courtesy is usually better than legal action:

A right minded poultryman will not permit his fowls to annoy his neighbors.

—John Henry Robinson, *Poultry-Craft*, 1899

Generally speaking, it is unwise to locate an egg farm within the limits of a city. The neighbors may not object to one or two crowing roosters and cackling hens but it may seem different to them if one hundred roosters and several thousand hens provide the concert. Furthermore, ground for complaint is easily found when even a single animal is kept in a city, let alone thousands of hens.

—Joseph Tumbach, *How I Made $10,000 in One Year with 4200 Hens*, 1919

FUN WITH EGGS
How to Play with Your Food

Most people are familiar with dyed or painted eggs, often given as gifts for Easter or New Year celebrations. Here are a few other eggish amusements, as recorded in the sixteenth century:

To make Eggs soft that you may put them into Glass Viols.

Infuse Eggs so long in sharp Vinegar until their shells grow soft; then thrust them into a narrow mouthed Glass, and pour cold water to them, and they will grow as hard as they were before, for Vinegar softens the Egg-shels, and water hardeneth them.

To write in Eggs.

Bruise Gals and Allum with Vinegar, until it be as thick as Ink, and with this write what you please upon an Egg, and when the writing is dried in the Sun, put the Egg into Salt pickle, and when it is dried, boyl it, and take away the shell, and you shall find the writing within the Egg. But if you cover the Egg with Wax and write upon it with a point of any sharp Iron making your Letters as deep as the shell, and then steep the Egg in Vinegar all night, and the next day take off the Wax, you shall see the Letters made by the Vinegar in the Egg very transparent.

To make an Egg bigger than a Mans head.

You shall separate ten or more Yelks and Whites of Eggs, and mingle the Yelks together, and put them into a bladder, and bind them round like an egg, put this into a Pot full of water and when you see it bubble, or when the Egg is grown hard take it out, and put in the Whites fitting it, as it ought to be, that the Yelks may be in the middle, then boyl it again. If you would have it covered with a shell make your shell thus. Grind white Egg shells washt clean, to very fine pouder, steep this in strong Vinegar until it grows soft or in distilled Vinegar; for if an Egg be left long in Vinegar, the shell will dissolve, and grows exceedingly tender, that it may easily be thrust into a narrow mouth'd Glass, as I said; when it is thrust in, fair water put to it will make it hard as it was before, that you will wonder at it. When the shells are dissolved like to an ointment, with a Pencill lay it on upon your Artificiall Egg, and let it grow hard in cold water, thus shall you make a true and naturall Egg.

To make an Egg flye up into the Ayre.

In May fill an Egg shell with May dew, and set it in the hot Sun at noon day, and the Sun will draw it up: and if sometimes it will hardly ascend it will be raised by help of a staff or Board to run up by.

—Johann Jacob Wecker, *Eighteen Books of the Secrets of Art & Nature*, 1582

PARTING ADVICE

Instructions for Beginning Chicken Keepers

RULES FOR SUCCESS

First, never getting tired.

Second, mastering the art or science of brooding chicks.

Third, renewing at least 60 per cent of the flock each year.

Fourth, concentrating on one particular branch of the work and keeping everlastingly at it.

Fifth, keeping accurate records and accounts.

Sixth, asking the giver of advice for his practical experience . . . before acting on it.

Seventh, disregarding the clock so far as the 8-hour day is concerned.

—Joseph Tumbach, *How I Made $10,000 in One Year with 4200 Hens,* 1919

THE HEN THAT HATCHED DUCKS

By Harriet Beecher Stowe (1867)

Once there was a nice young hen that we will call Mrs. Feathertop. She was a hen of most excellent family, being a direct descendant of the Bolton Grays, and as pretty a young fowl as you could wish to see of a summer's day. She was, moreover, as fortunately situated in life as it was possible for a hen to be. She was bought by young Master Fred Little John, with four or five family connections of hers, and a lively young cock, who was held to be as brisk a scratcher and as capable a head of a family as any half-dozen sensible hens could desire.

I can't say that at first Mrs. Feathertop was a very sensible hen. She was very pretty and lively, to be sure, and a great favourite with Master Bolton Gray Cock, on account of her bright eyes, her finely shaded feathers, and certain saucy dashing ways that she had which seemed greatly to take his fancy. But old Mrs. Scratchard, living in the neighbouring yard, assured all the neighbourhood that Gray Cock was a fool for thinking so much of that flighty young thing; that she had not the smallest notion how to get on in life, and thought of nothing in the world but her own pretty feathers.

"Wait till she comes to have chickens," said Mrs. Scratchard; "then you will see. I have brought up ten broods myself—as likely and respectable chickens as ever were a blessing to society—and I think I ought to know a good hatcher and brooder when I see her; and I know THAT fine piece of trumpery, with her white feathers tipped with gray, never will come down to family life. SHE scratch for chickens! Bless me, she never did anything in all her days but run round and eat the worms which somebody else scratched up for her."

When Master Bolton Gray heard this he crowed very loudly, like a cock of spirit, and declared that old Mrs. Scratchard was envious, because she had lost all her own tail-feathers, and looked more like a worn-out old feather-duster than a respectable hen, and that therefore she was filled with sheer envy of anybody that was young and pretty. So young Mrs. Feathertop cackled gay defiance at her busy rubbishy neighbour, as she sunned herself under the bushes on fine June afternoons.

Now Master Fred Little John had been allowed to have these hens by his mamma on the condition that he would build their house himself, and take all the care of it; and to do Master Fred justice, he executed the job in a small way quite creditably. He chose a sunny sloping bank covered with a thick growth of bushes, and erected there a nice little hen-house with two glass windows, a little door, and a good pole for his family to roost on. He made, moreover, a row of nice little boxes with hay in them for nests, and he bought three or four little smooth white china eggs to put in them, so that, when his hens DID lay, he might carry off their eggs without their being missed. This hen-house stood in a little grove that sloped down to

IMPERIAL EGG FOOD.

EGG FOOD MAKES CHICKENS LIVELY

DANGER

F.C.STURTEVANT HARTFORD CT U.S.

EGG FOOD

a wide river, just where there was a little cove which reached almost to the hen-house.

This situation inspired one of Master Fred's boy advisers with a new scheme in relation to his poultry enterprise. "Hallo! I say, Fred," said Tom Seymour, "you ought to raise ducks; you've got a capital place for ducks there."

"Yes; but I've bought HENS, you see," said Freddy; "so it's no use trying."

"No use! Of course there is. Just as if your hens couldn't hatch ducks' eggs. Now you just wait till one of your hens wants to sit, and you put ducks' eggs under her, and you'll have a family of ducks in a twinkling. You can buy ducks' eggs a plenty of old Sam under the hill. He always has hens hatch his ducks."

So Freddy thought it would be a good experiment, and informed his mother the next morning that he intended to furnish the ducks for the next Christmas dinner and when she wondered how he was to come by them, he said mysteriously, "Oh, I will show you how," but did not further explain himself. The next day he went with Tom Seymour and made a trade with old Sam, and gave him a middle-aged jack-knife for eight of his ducks' eggs. Sam, by-the-by, was a woolly-headed old negro man, who lived by the pond hard by, and who had long cast envying eyes on Fred's jack-knife, because it was of extra fine steel, having been a Christmas present the year before. But Fred knew very well there were any number more of jack-knives where that came from, and that, in order to get a new one, he must dispose of the old; so he made the purchase and came home rejoicing.

Now about this time Mrs. Feathertop, having laid her eggs daily with great credit to herself, notwithstanding Mrs. Scratchard's predictions, began to find herself suddenly attacked with nervous symptoms. She lost her gay spirits, grew dumpish and morose, stuck up her feathers in a bristling way, and pecked at her neighbours if they did so much as look at her. Master Gray Cock was greatly concerned, and went to old Dr. Peppercorn, who looked solemn, and recommended an infusion of angle-worms, and said he would look in on the patient twice a day till she was better.

"Gracious me, Gray Cock!" said old Goody Kertarkut, who had been lolling at the corner as he passed, "ain't you a fool?—cocks always are fools. Don't you know what's the matter with your wife? She wants to sit, that's all; and you just let her sit. A fiddlestick for Dr. Peppercorn! Why, any good old hen that has brought up a family knows more than a doctor about such things. You just go home and tell her to sit if she wants to, and behave herself."

When Gray Cock came home, he found that Master Freddy had been before him, and had established Mrs. Feathertop upon eight nice eggs, where she was sitting in gloomy grandeur. He tried to make a little affable conversation with her, and to relate his interview with the doctor and Goody Kertarkut; but she was morose and sullen, and only pecked at him now and then in a very sharp, unpleasant way. So after a few more efforts to make himself agreeable he left her, and went out promenading with the captivating Mrs. Red Comb, a charming young Spanish widow, who had just been imported into the neighbouring yard.

"Bless my soul," said he, "you've no idea how cross my wife is."

"O you horrid creature!" said Mrs. Red Comb. "How little you feel for the weaknesses of us poor hens!"

"On my word, ma'am," said Gray Cock, "you do me injustice. But when a hen gives way to temper, ma'am, and no longer meets her husband with a smile—when she even pecks at him whom she is bound to honour and obey—"

"Horrid monster! talking of obedience! I should say, sir, you came straight from Turkey." And Mrs. Red Comb tossed her head with a most bewitching air, and pretended to run away; and old Mrs. Scratchard looked out of her coop and called to Goody Kertarkut,—

"Look how Mr. Gray Cock is flirting with that widow. I always knew she was a baggage."

"And his poor wife left at home alone," said Goody Kertarkut. "It's the way with 'em all!"

"Yes, yes," said Dame Scratchard, "she'll know what real life is now, and she won't go about holding her head so high, and looking down on her practical neighbours that have raised families."

"Poor thing! what'll she do with a family?" said Goody Kertarkut.

"Well, what business have such young flirts to get married?" said Dame Scratchard. "I don't expect she'll raise a single chick; and there's Gray Cock flirting about, fine as ever. Folks didn't do so when I was young. I'm sure my husband knew what treatment a sitting hen ought to have,—poor old Long Spur! he never minded a peck or so now and then. I must say these modern fowls ain't what fowls used to be."

Meanwhile the sun rose and set, and Master Fred was almost the only friend and associate of poor little Mrs.

Feathertop, whom he fed daily with meal and water, and only interrupted her sad reflections by pulling her up occasionally to see how the eggs were coming on.

At last "Peep, peep, peep," began to be heard in the nest, and one little downy head after another poked forth from under the feathers, surveying the world with round, bright, winking eyes; and gradually the brood were hatched, and Mrs. Feathertop arose, a proud and happy mother, with all the bustling, scratching, care-taking instincts of family-life warm within her breast. She clucked and scratched, and cuddled the little downy bits of things as handily and discreetly as a seven-year-old hen could have done, exciting thereby the wonder of the community.

Master Gray Cock came home in high spirits, and complimented her; told her she was looking charmingly once more, and said, "Very well, very nice," as he surveyed the young brood. So that Mrs. Feathertop began to feel the world going well with her, when suddenly in came Dame Scratchard and Goody Kertarkut to make a morning call.

"Let's see the chicks," said Dame Scratchard.

"Goodness me," said Goody Kertarkut, "what a likeness to their dear papa!"

"Well, but bless me, what's the matter with their bills?" said Dame Scratchard.

"Why, my dear, these chicks are deformed! I'm sorry for you, my dear; but it's all the result of your inexperience. You ought to have eaten pebble-stones with your meal when you were sitting. Don't you see, Dame Kertarkut, what bills they have? That'll increase, and they'll be frightful!"

"What shall I do?" said Mrs. Feathertop, now greatly alarmed.

"Nothing, as I know of," said Dame Scratchard, "since you didn't come to me before you sat. I could have told you all about it. Maybe it won't kill 'em, but they'll always be deformed."

And so the gossips departed, leaving a sting under the pin-feathers of the poor little hen mamma, who began to see that her darlings had curious little spoon-bills, different from her own, and to worry and fret about it.

"My dear," she said to her spouse, "do get Dr. Peppercorn to come in and look at their bills, and see if anything can be done."

Dr. Peppercorn came in, and put on a monstrous pair of spectacles, and said, "Hum! ha! extraordinary case; very singular."

"Did you ever see anything like it, doctor?" said both parents in a breath.

"I've read of such cases. It's a calcareous enlargement of the vascular bony tissue, threatening ossification," said the doctor.

"Oh, dreadful! Can it be possible?" shrieked both parents. "Can anything be done?"

"Well, I should recommend a daily lotion made of mosquitoes' horns and bicarbonate of frogs' toes, together with a powder, to be taken morning and night, of muriate of fleas. One thing you must be careful about: they must never wet their feet, nor drink any water."

"Dear me, doctor, I don't know what I SHALL do, for they seem to have a particular fancy for getting into water."

"Yes, a morbid tendency often found in these cases of bony tumification of the vascular tissue of the mouth; but you must resist it, ma'am, as their life depends upon it." And with that Dr. Peppercorn glared gloomily on the young ducks, who were stealthily poking the objectionable little spoon-bills out from under their mother's feathers.

After this poor Mrs. Feathertop led a weary life of it; for the young fry were as healthy and enterprising a brood of young ducks as ever carried saucepans on the end of their noses, and they most utterly set themselves against the doctor's prescriptions, murmured at the muriate of fleas and the bicarbonate of frogs' toes, and took every opportunity to waddle their little ways down to the mud and water which was in their near vicinity. So their bills grew larger and larger, as did the rest of their bodies, and family government grew weaker and weaker.

"You'll wear me out, children, you certainly will," said poor Mrs. Feathertop.

"You'll go to destruction, do ye hear?" said Master Gray Cock.

"Did you ever see such frights as poor Mrs. Feathertop has got?" said Dame Scratchard. "I knew what would come of HER family—all deformed, and with a dreadful sort of madness which makes them love to shovel mud with those shocking spoon-bills of theirs."

"It's a kind of idiocy," said Goody Kertarkut. "Poor things! they can't be kept from the water, nor made to take powders, and so they get worse and worse."

"I understand it's affecting their feet so that they can't walk, and a dreadful sort of net is growing between their toes. What a shocking visitation!"

"She brought it on herself," said Dame Scratchard. "Why didn't she come to me before she sat? She was always an upstart, self-conceited thing; but I'm sure I pity her."

Meanwhile the young ducks throve apace. Their necks grew glossy, like changeable green and gold satin, and though they would not take the doctor's medicine, and would waddle in the mud and water—for which they always felt themselves to be very naughty ducks—yet they grew quite vigorous and hearty. At last one day the whole little tribe waddled off down to the bank of the river. It was a beautiful day, and the river was dancing and dimpling and winking as the little breezes shook the trees that hung over it.

"Well," said the biggest of the little ducks, "in spite of Dr. Peppercorn, I can't help longing for the water. I don't believe it is going to hurt me; at any rate, here goes," and in he plumped, and in went every duck after him, and they threw out their great brown feet as cleverly as if they had taken swimming lessons all their lives, and sailed off on the river, away, away among the ferns, under the pink azaleas, through reeds and rushes, and arrow-heads and pickerel-weed, the happiest ducks that ever were born; and soon they were quite out of sight.

"Well, Mrs. Feathertop, this is a dispensation!" said Mrs. Scratchard. "Your children are all drowned at last, just as I knew they'd be. The old music-teacher, Master Bullfrog, that lives down in Water-Dock Lane, saw 'em all plump madly into the water together this morning. That's what comes of not knowing how to bring up a family!"

Mrs. Feathertop gave only one shriek and fainted dead away, and was carried home on a cabbage-leaf; and Mr. Gray Cock was sent for, where he was waiting on Mrs. Red Comb through the squash-vines.

"It's a serious time in your family, sir," said Goody Kertarkut, "and you ought to be at home supporting your wife. Send for Dr. Peppercorn without delay."

Now as the case was a very dreadful one, Dr. Peppercorn called a council from the barn-yard of the squire, two miles off, and a brisk young Dr. Partlett appeared, in a fine suit of brown and gold, with tail-feathers like meteors. A fine young fellow he was, lately from Paris, with all the modern scientific improvements fresh in his head.

When he had listened to the whole story, he clapped his spur into the ground, and leaning back laughed so loudly that all the cocks in the neighbourhood crowed.

Mrs. Feathertop rose up out of her swoon, and Mr. Gray Cock was greatly enraged.

"What do you mean, sir, by such behaviour in the house of mourning?"

"My dear sir, pardon me; but there is no occasion for mourning. My dear madam, let me congratulate you. There is no harm done. The simple matter is, dear madam, you have been under a hallucination all along. The neighbourhood and my learned friend the doctor have all made a mistake in thinking that these children of yours were hens at all. They are ducks, ma'am, evidently ducks, and very finely-formed ducks I daresay."

At this moment a quack was heard, and at a distance the whole tribe were seen coming waddling home, their feathers gleaming in green and gold, and they themselves in high good spirits.

"Such a splendid day as we have had!" they all cried in a breath. "And we know now how to get our own living; we can take care of ourselves in future, so you need have no further trouble with us."

"Madam," said the doctor, making a bow with an air which displayed his tail-feathers to advantage, "let me congratulate you on the charming family you have raised. A finer brood of young, healthy ducks I never saw. Give me your claw, my dear friend," he said, addressing the eldest son. "In our barn-yard no family is more respected than that of the ducks."

And so Madam Feathertop came off glorious at last. And when after this the ducks used to go swimming up and down the river like so many nabobs among the admiring hens, Dr. Peppercorn used to look after them and say, "Ah, I had the care of their infancy!" and Mr. Gray Cock and his wife used to say, "It was our system of education did that!"

To Raise Poultry—[Being a letter written to a Poultry Society that had conferred a complimentary membership upon the author]
By Mark Twain (c. 1870)

Seriously, from early youth I have taken an especial interest in the subject of poultry-raising, and so this membership touches a ready sympathy in my breast. Even as a schoolboy, poultry-raising was a study with me, and I may say without egotism that as early as the age of seventeen I was acquainted with all the best and speediest methods of raising chickens, from raising them off a roost by burning lucifer matches under their noses, down to lifting them off a fence on a frosty night by insinuating the end of a warm board under their heels. By the time I was twenty years old, I really suppose I had raised more poultry than any one individual in all the section round about there. The very chickens came to know my talent by and by. The youth of both sexes ceased to paw the earth for worms, and old roosters that came to crow, "remained to pray," when I passed by.

I have had so much experience in the raising of fowls that I cannot but think that a few hints from me might be useful to the society. The two methods I have already touched upon are very simple, and are only used in the raising of the commonest class of fowls; one is for summer, the other for winter. In the one case you start out with a friend along about eleven o'clock on a summer's night (not later, because in some states—especially in California and Oregon—chickens always rouse up just at midnight and crow from ten to thirty minutes, according to the ease or difficulty they experience in getting the public waked up), and your friend carries with him a sack. Arrived at the henroost (your neighbor's, not your own), you light a match and hold it under first one and then another pullet's nose until they are willing to go into that bag without making any trouble about it. You then return home, either taking the bag with you or leaving it behind, according as circumstances shall dictate. N.B.—I have seen the time when it was eligible and appropriate to leave the sack behind and walk off with considerable velocity, without ever leaving any word where to send it.

In the case of the other method mentioned for raising poultry, your friend takes along a covered vessel with a charcoal fire in it, and you carry a long slender plank. This is a frosty night, understand. Arrived at the tree, or fence, or other henroost (your own if you are an idiot), you warm the end of your plank in your friend's fire vessel, and then raise it aloft and ease it up gently against a slumbering chicken's foot. If the subject of

your attentions is a true bird, he will infallibly return thanks with a sleepy cluck or two, and step out and take up quarters on the plank, thus becoming so conspicuously accessory before the fact to his own murder as to make it a grave question in our minds as it once was in the mind of Blackstone, whether he is not really and deliberately, committing suicide in the second degree. [But you enter into a contemplation of these legal refinements subsequently not then.]

When you wish to raise a fine, large, donkey voiced Shanghai rooster, you do it with a lasso, just as you would a bull. It is because he must be choked, and choked effectually, too. It is the only good, certain way, for whenever he mentions a matter which he is cordially interested in, the chances are ninety-nine in a hundred that he secures somebody else's immediate attention to it too, whether it day or night.

The Black Spanish is an exceedingly fine bird and a costly one. Thirty-five dollars is the usual figure and fifty a not uncommon price for a specimen. Even its eggs are worth from a dollar to a dollar and a half apiece, and yet are so unwholesome that the city physician seldom or never orders them for the workhouse. Still I have once or twice procured as high as a dozen at a time for nothing, in the dark of the moon. The best way to raise the Black Spanish fowl is to go late in the evening and raise coop and all. The reason I recommend this method is that, the birds being so valuable, the owners do not permit them to roost around promiscuously, they put them in a coop as strong as a fireproof safe and keep it in the kitchen at night. The method I speak of is not always a bright and satisfying success, and yet there are so many little articles of *vertu* about a kitchen, that if you fail on the coop you can generally bring away something else. I brought away a nice steel trap one night, worth ninety cents.

But what is the use in my pouring out my whole intellect on this subject? I have shown the Western New York Poultry Society that they have taken to their bosom a party who is not a spring chicken by any means, but a man who knows all about poultry, and is just as high up in the most efficient methods of raising it as the president of the institution himself. I thank these gentlemen for the honorary membership they have conferred upon me, and shall stand at all times ready and willing to testify my good feeling and my official zeal by deeds as well as by this hastily penned advice and information. Whenever they are ready to go to raising poultry, let them call for me any evening after eleven o'clock.

ACKNOWLEDGMENTS
AND NOTE ON SOURCES

This book began at the Huntington Library in San Marino, California, where curators in every department helped me find material for what they all agreed was a "most amusing" topic. Further research in the collections of Northwestern University, the Lenhardt Library at the Chicago Botanic Garden, the University of Chicago, the Newberry Library, and the Library of Congress revealed more treasures, and I am very grateful to the wonderful librarians and archivists at all these places. Special thanks go to Sarah Keyes, Dan Lewis, David Mihaly, Donald Opitz, and Mary Terrall, for pointing me to sources I would never have discovered on my own, and to Barbara Newman for translating Latin texts. Kristin King-Ries graciously read this book at different stages, offering sage suggestions and saving me from embarrassing errors. I am more grateful than I can say to Carl Smith, Lucia Smith, Jeremy Smith, and Crissie McMullan, all of whom helped bring both words and pictures into line while listening to far more tales from the chicken yard than they had ever expected to hear. Rob McQuilkin and Christina Shideler recognized the charm of this quirky collection, and Holly Rubino brought it into being; to all three, many thanks.

My greatest debt is to the learned chicken enthusiasts who wrote down their observations of this most available and yet most mysterious domestic bird. I am equally indebted to the scribes and translators who preserved the earliest works, as noted below. Most of the illustrations in this book are from the nineteenth century, when raising chickens was considered an art, a science, and a practical necessity; great praise is due to the many artists, both famous and unknown, who devoted themselves to poultry portraiture in an age when that was a popular art.

Authors are cited after every extract, but their translators deserve mention:

Ulisse Aldrovandi, the first professor of natural science at the ancient University of Bologna, published his great compendium of bird lore, *Ornithologiae,* in 1599. The translations quoted here are from Edmund Saul Dixon's *Treatise on the History and Management of Ornamental and Domestic Poultry* (Philadelphia: E. H. Butler & Co., 1853) and from R. L. Lind's *The Ornithology of Ulisse Aldrovandi* (Norman, OK: University of Oklahoma Press, 1963).

Junius Oderatus Columella was a Roman military commander and agriculturalist of the first century. His book *Of Husbandry* (*De Re Rustica*) dates from the middle of the first century, most likely the year 65 AD. The anonymous translation cited here was published in London in 1745.

Athanasius Kircher, a German Jesuit of many interests, spent most of his life in Rome, where he published *The Great Art of Light and Shadow* (*Ars Magna Lucis et Umbrae*) in 1646. The translation here is courtesy of Barbara Newman.

Pliny the Elder's *Natural History* (*Naturalis Historia*) was published shortly before his sudden death during the eruption of Mt. Vesuvius in 79 AD. Citations are from Philemon Holland's 1601 translation, *The Historie of the World*, London.

René Antoine Ferchault de Réaumer's *Art de faire éclorre et délever en tout saison des oiseaux Domestiques de toutes espèces* was published in Paris in 1749 and quickly translated into several languages. The anonymous translation cited here, *On the Art of Hatching and Bringing Up Domestic Fowls*, was published by C. Davis, A. Millar, and J. Nourse, London: 1750.

Marcus Terentius Varro, a Roman military commander, landholder, and prolific writer (most of whose works are lost), wrote *Country Matters* (*De Re Rustica*) some time in the first century BC. The translation cited here, by "a Virginia Farmer," is *Roman Farm Management: The Treatises of Cato and Varro*, New York: The MacMillan Company, 1913.

Johann Jacob Wecker's *De Secretis Libri XVII* first appeared in Latin in Switzerland in 1582. The edition cited here, *Eighteen Books of the Secrets of Art and Nature*, was translated into English and "augmented" by R. Read, London: 1660.

ILLUSTRATION CREDITS

The illustrations in this book are the work of multiple artists, many of them anonymous, whose efforts provided both style and accuracy in the days before color photography. Printing plates for engravings and lithographs were used repeatedly, so the same images often appeared in multiple publications. The credits below note where these particular examples were found.

Courtesy of Library of Congress Prints and
    Photographs Division, Washington, D.C.:
    Pages x, 19, 51

Reproduced by permission of the Huntington
    Library, San Marino, California:
    Pages 4, 26, 35, 58, 61, 81, 83, 100, 120, 123, 143

The American Agriculturist, New York: Orange Judd &
    Company, May 1869:
    Pages 102, 105, 106, 109, 129, 136
    Reproduced by permission of the Rare Book
    Collection of the Lenhardt Library of the
    Chicago Botanic Garden.

The American Standard of Perfection, American Poultry
Association, 1910:
Page 39

Fourth Annual Catalog, The Sure Hatch Incubator
Company, Clay Center, NE: 1901:
Page 78

*Illustrated Annual Register of Rural Affairs for 1861-2-3,
Vol. III*, Albany, NY: Luther Tucker & Son,
1864:
Pages 11, 57, 72
Reproduced by permission of the Rare Book
Collection of the Lenhardt Library of the
Chicago Botanic Garden.

Profits in Poultry, New York: Orange Judd Company,
1895:
Pages 55, 157

George P. Burnham, *The History of the Hen Fever*,
Boston: James French and Company, 1855:
Pages iii, 23, 99

R. E. Jones and Theo. Hewes, *From Shell to Showroom*,
Indianapolis, IN: Inland Poultry Journal, 1903:
Pages 49, 52, 65, 75

H. H. Stoddard, *How to Feed Fowls*, Hartford, CT:
1882:
Page 48

Lewis Wright, *The Illustrated Book of Poultry**, London,
New York, Toronto, Melbourne: Cassell and
Company, Ltd, 1890:
Pages 2, 7, 12, 14, 15, 17, 20, 29, 30, 34, 40, 42, 43,
45, 51, 69, 70, 73, 90, 96, 110, 115, 117, 118, 124,
127, 132, 134, 139, 140, 156, 158, 163, 166

Lewis Wright, *The Practical Poultry Keeper**, London,
New York, Toronto, Melbourne: Cassell and
Company, Ltd, 1909:
Pages 46, 47, 128, 131

*color illustrations by J. Ludlow